REMEMBER THE DAYS OF OLD

# Foundations series

Testifying to the faith and creativity of the Orthodox Christian
Church, the Foundations series draws upon the riches of its
tradition to address the modern world. These survey texts are
suitable both for preliminary inquiry and deeper investigation,
in the classroom and for personal study.

Peter C. Bouteneff
*Series Editor*

BOOK 1
*Stages on Life's Way: Orthodox Thinking on Bioethics*
by John and Lyn Breck

BOOK 2
*Seeds of the Word: Orthodox Thinking on Other Religions*
by John Garvey

BOOK 3
*Sweeter Than Honey: Orthodox Thinking on Dogma and Truth*
by Peter C. Bouteneff

BOOK 4
*Living in God's Creation: Orthodox Perspectives on Ecology*
by Elizabeth Theokritoff

BOOK 5
*Fellow Workers with God: Orthodox Thinking on Theosis*
by Norman Russell

BOOK 6
*Remember the Days of Old: Orthodox Thinking on the Patristic Heritage*
by Augustine Casiday

BOOK 6 OF THE FOUNDATIONS SERIES

# Remember the Days of Old

## ORTHODOX THINKING ON THE PATRISTIC HERITAGE

*Augustine Casiday*

ST VLADIMIR'S SEMINARY PRESS
YONKERS, NEW YORK
2014

Library of Congress PCN

2014934159

© 2014 BY AUGUSTINE CASIDAY

ST VLADIMIR'S SEMINARY PRESS
575 Scarsdale Rd, Yonkers, NY 10707
1-800-204-2665
www.svspress.com



ISSN 1556-9837
ISBN 978-0-88141-491-2

For Andrew Louth,
teacher, priest, friend
ἐπαξίως εὐφημοῦμέν σε· ὑπάρχεις γάρ
καθηγητής, ὡς τά θεία σαφῶν

*Remember the days of old, consider the years
of many generations: ask thy father, and he
will shew thee; thy elders, and they will tell thee.*
Deut 32.7


*History is powerful in forming minds because
it forms them without the mind being conscious
that it is being formed, and the reader thinks
himself to be only following a story.*
Owen Chadwick,
*The Secularization of the European
Mind in the Nineteenth Century*

# CONTENTS

# FOREWORD

Metropolitan Anthony (Bloom) once called in an Orthodox scholar to comment on an article she wrote about women's roles in the Church. She asked him whether he thought that her essay went too far. He replied, "No, the problem is that you didn't go far enough!" He went on to give her an image: "The Orthodox Church is like a great tree. Its roots run deep into the past, and this is what gives the foundation. But its branches must go upward and outward."

This image powerfully evokes the challenge to which serious Christians are called: to be faithful at once to the past and to the present. The faith of the orthodox Christian is "apostolic," in that it is continuous with the faith of the first-century apostles. But to be truly apostolic it must be sent into the world, speaking to each new age. We cite this objective so often that it can sound banal, yet to actually be true to the ancient expressions of faith, and to really make them breathe and live today speaking to our questions, can be extremely difficult. This, evidently, is why it is so easy to turn "ancient faith" or "traditional theology" into an empty slogan, or at the other extreme to relegate it to an impenetrable ivory tower. The challenge is clear, but the means of negotiating it are not. How does one simultaneously keep deep roots in the ground of tradition, while allowing the branches of that same tree to grow freely and fearlessly?

The challenge demands a realistic approach to the past. Simply to foist our questions and problems on the Fathers of the first millennium won't do: their contexts—their questions and their opponents—were different. As Fr Sergius Bulgakov summarized succinctly, "One cannot seek in the writings of one period answers to the questions inherent in another."[1] How, then, can we appeal to the past for guidance?

The answer lies in devoting ourselves to understanding the questions, dilemmas, and crises being addressed by the Church Fathers. We must seek to understand what they were grappling with, how they approached the life of the Church, how they themselves consulted the past. We have to be cognizant both of the continuity between their questions and crises and our own, as well as the disconnects. Some areas require not only a linguistic but also a conceptual translation in order to be accurate and intelligible. The only meaningful way to glean from their teaching is to treat the Fathers comprehensively, truly to get to know them within their time, to the extent possible.

The goal of the present volume is both to emphasize the necessity of this task, and to put us squarely on the way to addressing it. Beginning with the basic inquiry of what it means to accord the ancient writers' authority—as it were affiliating them, or *adopting* them as fathers—the reader is invited to join on a journey to many new places, as well as to ones we thought we knew, but didn't really. Among these forays is an exploration of how the fathers themselves consulted the past and read each other, as well

---

[1] "Dogma and Dogmatic Theology," in Michael Plekon, ed., *Tradition Alive: On the Church and the Christian Life in Our Time* (Sheed & Ward/Rowman & Littlefield, 2003), 67–80 (71).

as an inquiry into what we may reasonably expect from theological (symbolic) language. Throughout we are given vivid examples from the past, as well as from modern attempts (successful and not) in appropriating it. We are thus led to important and practical conclusions about the most profitable and holistic ways to root our understanding in tradition, so that the branches and leaves of our faith push upward and outward, bearing fruit.

One often says about a book, usually with unrealistic hopes, that it will benefit beginning students as well as scholars. This book makes good on that promise: it will inform *anyone* who wants to grapple with how we treat the past and its authoritative voices. Beginners will encounter a first-rate thinker writing comprehensibly and accessibly. Advanced patristic scholars will be guaranteed to come away from this book with new insights and challenging arguments.

Augustine Casiday challenges everyone, especially us Orthodox Christians, who may believe that we have a privileged access to the ancient Church. He warns us how easily this can lead to a false security, an insularity. It can lead us to mistake prejudices for insights. What all of us should seek is "an honest engagement with the present that is informed by an awareness of the past that is critical, scrupulous, and honest" (p. 42). This book will affirm and immeasurably assist that pursuit.

—Peter Bouteneff

# INTRODUCTION

I f the blood of the martyrs is the seed of the Church, the legacy of the Fathers is the fruit of the Church. Orthodox Christians take special pride in their fidelity to this legacy, but rarely consider what this fidelity might mean. Often, the patristic heritage is taken for granted. The consequences are regrettable for Orthodox scholars of church history and historical theology, but also (perhaps even especially) for Orthodox who are simply interested in making that heritage their own. This book aims to promote critical reflection on Orthodox tradition as exemplified by the words of the Fathers, by focusing primarily on their writings, but also by drawing on the cultural history of Eastern Christianity. It does so in the belief that such critical engagement, when attempted with honesty, humility, and above all filial respect, can only be to the good.

Certain intellectual steps ought to be taken to promote a healthy and robust engagement with the past. To foster a wholesome and sustainable habit of appropriating the legacy of our fathers and mothers, brothers and sisters in the faith, we need to draw attention to some of the ways modern developments in history and philosophy can deepen readers' understanding of patristic literature. Because this book's purpose will be to encourage that kind of deeper understanding, it will aim first and foremost to be practical. It aims to motivate readers to turn to ancient Christian sources with an expectation that is enriched and informed. For that reason, the book does *not* present a patrology or an outline of the development of Christian dogma. Such works are readily available. Besides, even though patristic doctrine has been extremely important in guaranteeing the kind of interest that has led to the study, preservation, and promotion of patristic literature as a whole, there is far more to the patristic heritage than doctrinal theology. For that reason, the subject matter treated here will not be restricted to doctrine alone.

It may be helpful to say a word about avoiding a narrow preoccupation with doctrine. First, within the tradition of catholic orthodoxy, the formation of classical Christian doctrine is at least as much concerned to eliminate errors as it is to specify the content of the Christian message. Already in the earliest days of Christianity, we find evidence of some teachings being condemned and countered by alternate teachings. Hence, the exhortation to Timothy:

> Preach the word; be instant in season, out of season; reprove, rebuke, exhort with all long suffering and doctrine. For the time will come when they will not endure sound doctrine; but after their own lusts shall they heap to themselves teachers, having itching ears; and they shall turn away their ears from the truth, and shall be turned unto fables (2 Tim 4.2–4).

As we see in this passage, proclamation, evangelization, and apology stand alongside redressing error as valuable ways to promote "sound doctrine." There is no limit in principle to the modes of speech that can communicate Christian doctrine. But, in historical terms, the enduring statements of ancient Christian teaching about Jesus Christ, the Holy Trinity, and the Mother of Our Lord are responses that were framed during crises. Generally speaking, doctrines were not articulated because they were the inevitable implications of earlier doctrines, nor were they expressed in anticipation of problems that might arise (which is why the results are often unsatisfying when theologians scour texts from fourth-century Anatolia in search of answers to the problems of twenty-first century America).

A second reason not to restrict our attention to doctrinal theology is that doctrines tend to bear the imprints of the controversies that gave rise to them. Consider the following features that recur during controversies:

- the dense use of technical vocabulary;

- the limited range of the discussion (which is often imposed for practical considerations);

- a cluster of rhetorical features—such as caustic personal attacks, disparaging and racist allegations of "Jewishness," or other forms of vilification—that aim to create sharp demarcations and separate groups within what an outsider to the debate might otherwise consider a single community; and

- arguments that are more vindictive than explanatory and sometimes seriously flawed for that very reason.

I have deliberately exaggerated that list to accentuate some of the most repellent characteristics that can be found in treatises, letters, and conciliar acts from the ancient church. I exaggerate to make a point: disputation is a very distinctive type of interaction, and it does not necessarily provide the best context for offering up a fitting response in thanksgiving for the wonders wrought by God. To point this out is in no way to devalue the importance of an orthodox profession of faith, perhaps especially professions hard won. I am not trying to suggest, for example, that the doctrinal substructure of an orthodox profession is arbitrary or endlessly revisable or relevant only for the study of antiquity. I am suggesting rather that the technical and polemical nature of patristic disputation *alone* is insufficient to carry the joy and glory of the Gospel.

I mentioned some off-putting characteristics in patristic literature. Certainly, some modern scholars have expressed distaste for the features of that literature already mentioned. On a related note, other scholars are concerned that the articulation of orthodox doctrine necessarily implies the silencing of dissent, or perhaps merely diverging perspectives. We cannot deny that doctrinal theology does preclude some options, but this does not mean that orthodoxy is unduly restrictive. This brings us to a third point. The limitations of orthodox Christian doctrine are more apparent than real, because orthodox teaching points the Christian beyond itself to God. By the early Byzantine period, Greek patristic works show that doctrinal principles serve as the platform for the uppermost reaches of theology understood precisely as an encounter with God. It is therefore possible to speak of an "outward trajectory" of doctrinal theology. Doctrine points beyond its own formulations. Human words—even the words of Christian doctrine—do not and cannot exhaustively describe the human condition; how much less are they adequate to the divine reality? For that reason, it is necessary to attend to non-doctrinal and even non-verbal elements of the Christian inheritance.

From the third observation there follows a fourth and final reason to take a broad view of the patristic heritage, rather than focusing on patristic dogma. Dogmatic statements are assuredly a matter of great importance, but they are but one component of the legacy that ancient Christians bequeathed to moderns. A priority of this book is to promote the habit of acknowledging the complexity of the patristic heritage and, insofar as it is practical, of engaging with that heritage in its complexity. The multiple written forms of the tradition are easy to identify. They include the lives of saints ("hagiography"), poetry, sermons, occasional letters, pilgrims' travelogues, hymnody, autobiography, chronicles and histories, "centuries" (chains of multiply-interconnected "chapters," or brief and typically aphoristic statements), commentaries, prayers, handbooks, and collections of spiritual and monastic counsel. Nor does the literary heritage exhaustively account for the tradition as a whole. We also inherit from earlier generations of Christians their material culture (icons, murals, statues, cathedrals, monasteries, baptisteries, manuscripts, reliquaries, liturgical furniture) and ritual forms (the Eucharist, baptism, catechism, specially designated times for prayer, blessings at numerous events of significance in the lives of the faithful). This book cannot pretend to offer complete coverage of any of those topics. Nevertheless, I will draw from the widest possible range in the following chapters. We cannot properly understand the precious doctrines that have been handed down from antiquity if we consider them in isolation from the patristic tradition as a whole.

Another feature of the book is that it will make use of ideas and develop suggestions that come from a range of later sources. Some of these will be academic texts; others, modern essays. The rationale for employing them is that the early Christians themselves vigorously engaged with secular culture and made use of it. We can think of this process without much exaggeration as the baptism of non-Christian antiquity. When St Augustine considered how Christians could fashion "ornaments" for the worship of God from the jewels of paganism, he recalled the Exodus of the children of Israel and memorably labeled the re-purposing of secular learning "despoiling the Egyptians." St Basil the Great's "Letter to youth on how they may profit from Greek learning" demonstrates a comparable impulse to defend self-consciously Christian involvement in education and in the transmission of classical Greek literature. These are merely two examples of a transformation that occurred throughout the Mediterranean world (and beyond) as a direct result of the ascendance of Christianity. The willingness to enter the public realm and to draw freely on contemporary culture was not just a clever way of getting the Christian message across to people who might otherwise have thought it too uncouth. It was a way of bearing witness to Christ to the general public in their own language. This willingness is one of the marks that distinguish Christians of the Great Church from sectarian Christians.

The same willingness to engage contemporary culture also helps account for the astounding vitality of patristic intellectual activity, since appropriation of the language of the public became one of the dynamos that drove Christian theology. As people think, and talk about what they are thinking, there inevitably emerge fresh conjunctions of words and contexts, opportunities and needs. As history continually unfolds Christians are presented with ever new occasions to bear witness to the Father through the Son by the Spirit. Early Christians responded to the situations they encountered, and the multiple ways in which they did so help us understand the development of Christian doctrine and tradition as a whole. Keeping in mind the ongoing need to communicate the good news effectively to others "in season, out of season," we see that the process never ground to a halt at any point. *Our responsibility to bear witness to Christ to our own contemporaries follows suit.* It is not fulfilled by the ancient formulation of the Nicene-Constantinopolitan Creed, by the Chalcedonian expression of orthodox Christology, by the restoration of icons in the Byzantine church, by the vindication of Gregory Palamas' hesychastic theology in the fourteenth century, or even by our own ability merely to recapitulate any of these teachings. We, too, participate in the ongoing need to communicate the good news effectively in our own time. It is only if we think that the process has somehow run into the sand that we become anxious about somehow "re-launching" it. A faithful adherence to the legacy of the Fathers includes faith in its vital dynamism and an acknowledgement of our own responsibility to continue within it.

There is no important sense in which ancient Christianity came to an end. We believe instead that it lives on through the ongoing reception and implementation of its legacy. Even so, we are obliged to recognize that bringing its heritage to bear faithfully and fruitfully in an age far removed from it is one of the most daunting challenges that faces us. I will suggest in some detail later that following the lead of the ancients themselves is at least a partial answer to this challenge, that we may do as they did, that we may give an answer for the hope that is within us, in terms that are intelligible and culturally meaningful. Creative fidelity to their practice justifies the use of ideas and language coming from other sources in the attempt to make their works available to modern readers.

* * *

To this point, I have somewhat abstractly described an open-ended project and indicated my hope that this book will make a contribution. An overview of the chapters to follow will help make things more concrete. Considering patristics for any length of time raises a preliminary question: what do we mean when we describe certain people as "fathers"? We will focus on this question in Chapter 1 ("What is the patristic heritage?"). We will consider first the dynamics of the relationship suggested by talking about men from the past as our "fathers." The first line of movement is to put ourselves in the role of their children. What does it mean to think of them as standing in that parental relation to us? In many respects, the parent's position in relation to the child is superior; does that hold true in this case as well? These questions take the parent as the chief point of reference in the relationship. We may also take the child as our point of reference. For there are curious and distinctive features to the relationship that are not otherwise apparent. Consider, for instance, the common form of non-biological parentage—adoption. Usually, the parent adopts a child; but in the special case we will discuss, the child adopts the parent, so to speak. Or rather, we *affiliate* ourselves. We as children take an active role, and this is a part of the relationship that needs to be taken seriously. Considering both of these vectors will help us understand the dynamics that characterize the relationship that we have with our Fathers in the Church.

Also in the first chapter, we will think about the heritage itself as the Christian culture we have inherited from our predecessors. Thinking about heritage in this way enables us to think through some of the problems that attach to "tradition." For reasons that we will consider in due course, the casual use of the expression "living tradition" has been criticized recently. The criticism is not in itself devastating, but it does merit a response because it identifies potential problems. Most of them have to do with a curious idea that "tradition" necessarily is mechanical and automatic (which means unthinking) and conservative (which is also a term of abuse in some quarters). Though it is true that carelessness sometimes results in unthinking repetition, the relationships that we will describe in this chapter are anything but careless and unthinking.

Throughout this chapter we will make use of some key ideas from H.-G. Gadamer's approach to philosophical hermeneutics, or interpretation. Those ideas will be complemented by themes drawn from other modern figures. These writers were not concerned with how Orthodox Christians stand in relation to the Fathers of the Church, yet their work offers invaluable assistance in thinking about how we understand and interpret the past. They also suggest a posture of openness to being challenged by historical sources and maturing as a result of those challenges—which, as we shall see, is entirely consistent with an orthodox approach to the saints.

Reflecting upon the patristic heritage that joins contemporary Orthodox Christians to ancient Christian saints prepares us for the major question of the second chapter: "How is it transmitted?" In response to that question, we will focus on the ways in which the patristic heritage is propagated and what happens along the way. There are many lines of transmission from past authors to present readers, and the process is rarely a smooth one. Happily, we have recourse to abundant evidence of that process at work in specific examples of later Fathers inheriting, then passing on, the thought of earlier Fathers: Vincent of Lérins' attitude toward Origen and toward Augustine, Maximus' explanation of Gregory of Nazianzus in his *Ambigua*, and Photios' response to patristic citations ostensibly supporting the filioque. What we find in these examples will lead us to a further refinement of the original question posed in this chapter.

Initially we asked how the heritage is transmitted. The case studies help us to think about how that heritage is *appropriated*. The difference between transmission and appropriation is a matter of which end of the process we focus on. It is similar to focusing first on fathers, then on their children. By looking not only to the originators but also to the recipients, we find that our role as recipients is not passive. Instead, we have an active part in affiliating ourselves to certain ancient Christians. What attitudes are most conducive to the successful transmission of the patristic heritage? We need to attend to the preparations—mental, perhaps, but especially spiritual—that enable us to take up the culture that has come down to us.

In the first two chapters, we observe how taking up the ancient heritage occurs within the Christian community. In the final two chapters, we consider the community itself. First, in Chapter 3, we will think about the network of symbols constructed from patristic sources and the roles that those patristic symbols play in Orthodox life. A historical survey will help us understand what a symbol is and what it does. Of particular interest is the fact that the symbol functions because of its *incompleteness*. Next we turn to the use of symbols in early Christianity, which includes not only recognizable signs but also statements of faith.

Whether verbal or visual, symbols of all sorts have significant social functions in creating and maintaining group identity. These social functions will be weighed in our reading of the Nicene-Constantinopolitan Creed and the significance that attaches to it. This path will take us to a fiercely contested point of theology—the affirmation in Western Christendom that the Holy Spirit proceeds from the Father *and from the Son*. Without attempting to settle an ancient controversy, we will instead consider the presuppositions about history and about the historical character of theology that are usually activated when that topic is debated.

Finally, in Chapter 4, we will look at some of the ways that the patristic legacy can promote or support modern Orthodox life in general. I will argue that fidelity to the patristic heritage means involving ourselves with the world around us and *not* sequestering ourselves in a patristic ghetto. That is, of course, easier said than done. There can be a poor fit between the source material and our modern needs, since the circumstances in which the originals were produced were different in important ways from our circumstances. Redeploying ancient material in the modern world is frankly hard work. But it can be done. I will suggest two examples. The first is how social outreach can be a mode of worshipping God. The second is how a modern spirituality malady can be identified by recourse to monastic insights. In both cases, I identify resources that can be used as part of a robust response to modern circumstances. My remarks about how those resources can be used will be provisional, of course, and not prescriptive. Again, it is not my purpose to institute a theological curriculum based on patristic sources. Instead, I am offering an encouragement to look to the rich tradition of the ancient Church so as to meet the demands and seize the opportunities of modern life.

*chapter one*

# WHAT IS THE PATRISTIC HERITAGE?

This book is an essay about the patristic heritage and its importance for contemporary Orthodox theology. Since, however, we Orthodox Christians are not alone in valuing highly the patristic heritage and since Orthodox Christianity is increasingly visible in the English-speaking world, I am writing with the hope that it may also be worthwhile reading for those who do not belong to an Orthodox Church. In any case, we need to pause at the start and to reflect on a question so fundamental that it might otherwise go unnoticed. Before we can consider the patristic heritage in a sustained way, we need to define both "patristic" and "heritage."

"Patristic" indicates that any given thing comes from or belongs to the "fathers" of the Church. (The English word *patristic* comes indirectly from the Latin word *pater* which, like the Greek πατήρ, means "father.") "Heritage" refers to that which is passed from one generation to the next, often within a family. From these two definitions, two important questions arise. The first is, what do we mean when we describe certain people as "fathers"? And the second: what is it that we are "inheriting" from them? As this chapter progresses, we shall see that these questions are not as simple as they might seem. In what follows, we will consider what it means for us to talk about some people from that past as "fathers" and to regard ourselves as their inheritors. In the course of this chapter, we will see how these questions are important and significant—and, along the way, I will introduce ideas and themes that will be used in subsequent chapters.

So first, we will consider two major implications of talking about historical figures as "fathers." Then we will direct our attention to the things that we inherit from those historical figures—that is, to the *heritage* itself. These considerations will prepare us for the somewhat more advanced topics that will be covered later in this book.

## The Fathers

When we talk about people from the past as "fathers" (or some-times, albeit rarely, as "mothers"), we are claiming a special kind of relationship to them. We are claiming them as parents and, at the same time, we are claiming to be their children. We can even say that we are *affiliating* ourselves to them, in the strongest, etymological sense of that word: we are *making ourselves their children*. This use of family language is not casual. Actually, it is extremely serious, even if frequent use keeps us from reflecting often enough (or deeply enough) on what it means.

We talk about spiritual fathers and about the holy Fathers—by which we basically mean the saints of the church, without limit-ing ourselves to any particular period of history—and we address priests and monks as "fathers." The fact that these kinship terms are extended in religious circumstances is not exceptional. They can also be applied to adoptive or foster parents, to great scientific or political innovators, or as a mark of affection to older people. Think of Galileo Galilei, the "father of modern astronomy," or the Founding Fathers of the United States. When we use the word "father" in these contexts, we are extending it well beyond the basic, biological sense, where it refers to the male who contributes twenty-three chromosomes toward the biological generation of a new human.

But biology is not the final word. In fact, Christians don't take biological fatherhood as basic. Taking inspiration from Ephesians 3.14–15, Christians think that every earthly (and even heavenly) example of fatherhood—πατριά—is named after the Father of Jesus Christ. In doing so, we affirm that every example of fatherhood that is worthy of the name in one way or another imitates the relationship of God the Father toward Jesus Christ. That divine relationship exemplifies fatherhood and, for that reason, it teaches us how to recognize basic attributes of fatherhood. Those basic attributes are the stable features that allow us to apply the term in a range of circumstances.

Even though we use the term "father" in various circumstances, we are reminded that the term applies, ultimately and most properly, to God the Father in relation to the Son. Our use of the term "father" resonates with theological significance. Now is not the time to trace closely the ways in which the divine meaning echoes when the word "father" is used in particular cases, but it is good to remember the term's theological ramifications. From time to time in the pages that follow, we will get our bearings by referring back to the divine fatherhood of God. For now, we need to turn back to the particular case of fatherhood that is implied by the term "patristic."

* * *

When we cast ourselves as children in relationship to the Fathers of the Church, two important consequences follow. The first of them comes from the fact that there is a basic inequality between the two parties. In other words, there is a fundamental disparity in the relationship of parents to children. We can see that this is so by noting how young children depend upon their parents. In the most basic sense, we see this kind of dependency in the ways that parents nurture, clothe, and clean their child who would otherwise be helpless. Acts of nurturing are by no means restricted *either* to the mother *or* to the father; the model of parental nourishing we are exploring is not at all centered on the father. The mother in all likelihood plays by far the greatest role in sustaining the child. This should be kept in mind when we talk, as convention obliges, of "fathers."

There is no denying that some aspects of the relationship of parent to child may be gender-specific. A father is incapable of suckling his child, after all, and the initial nurturing of the developing child is provided only in the mother's womb. Despite this gender-specifity, though, the parental relationship as such is not restricted to one gender or the other. Both a mother and a father are equally a parent. And thinking back to what we have already said about God being the model father, we will be aware that gender limitations do not apply to God even when the term "Father" is used. This awareness tells against the fact that conventional language (such as the language that we are using) has a gender-bias toward males. However, we are not by this awareness liberated to use language in whatever way we see fit.

A model of parental nurture comes to mind when we read of St Paul telling the Athenians, "For in him we live and move and have our being" (Acts 17.28). Likewise, when Christ speaks of his love for the Chosen People of God, he calls himself a hen and them chicks (Mt 23.37; Lk 13.34). These passages help us to recognize that our relationship with God is one of children depending for their very existence upon their parent. Initially physical, nurturing also includes the formation of character. Food to nourish the body, instruction and discipline to nourish the mind and soul: all these things are the natural obligation of parents to provide. As we move from nutritional sustenance and the protection of physical well being to more abstract (but certainly no less critical) forms of nourishment like education and moral training, we also move from considering the nuclear family in artificial isolation to thinking of the family as members of a *society*.

Education and moral training are social activities; they fit their beneficiary for life in society. Under ideal circumstances, moral formation and intellectual development are processes that never come to an end. Moral and intellectual growth continues throughout life, and can be compared to the constant needs for sustenance, shelter, and protection of the physical body. Both are relationships of ongoing dependence.

Some would instinctively resist the idea that dependence is a permanent feature of human life. They might reject it out of a sense of potential disgrace or irreconcilability with the ideal of an independent, mature, decision-making adult. Dependence is an affront to some deeply held political ideals. Similarly, we tend to use the word "dependency" to describe unhealthy emotional relationships, for example, situations in which one person completely relies upon another in a way that violates that person's natural dignity as a human. Or, one person could so totally dominate another that the other person's integrity is violated. Yet the threat of violence is by no means implied in every relationship where there is dependence or inequality.

Leaving aside political constructs and pathology, in order to understand how dependence continues into, and in fact throughout, adulthood, let us keep in mind how babies are dependent upon their parents and all people are dependent upon their societies.

Our dependence as children upon the Fathers of the Church is both a positive and persistent factor. It is not something that we outgrow as we mature. Instead, it is, if you like, a structural component of relating to them as their children. Even when an infant matures into childhood, adolescence, and then adulthood, the relationship remains. It doesn't remain the same; it matures, but the fact that children relate to their parents is constant, even as the character of the relationship flourishes and ripens. For this reason, we can talk about continuing to be sons and daughters of our Fathers, even into adulthood, growing in maturity without losing our relationship to them.

* * *

The second thing to consider about what it means when we affiliate ourselves to the Fathers of the church is how very specific the relationship is. We are not claiming to stand in a child's relationship to some abstract idea—"the Fathers" as a sort of undifferentiated pack of holy people. Instead, we are asserting a special kind of relationship with *certain* people from the past. Even if we do not have a definitive roster of the saints, an all-inclusive collection of saints' lives or the like, even if for all practical purposes we lack the formal procedures for canonization and promoting devotion to holy women and men that we see at work in the Roman Catholic Church, even if we consequently are willing to think of the host of the saints as very much an open group, even if we have liturgical catch-alls (services for "All Saints," or "All Saints of Greece" or "of Russia" or "of Great Britain," or "all the holy and God-bearing fathers and mothers who have shown forth in the ascetic life . . . "), we need to understand our generality and openness as a practical matter. There are only so many days on the calendar for commemorating saints; we forget some through the multitude of names; we rightly allow ample space for honoring and showing respect to God when we see evidence of God's love at work in the life of even the obscure and the unknown. But these concessions do not diminish the fact that each and every saint is known by name to God; they make up "a chosen nation, a royal priesthood," and not some anonymous crowd.

Thus, even though we do not pretend to know all the saints known to God, we do effectively make a selection when we talk about "the Fathers." Recognizing that our knowledge is imperfect, we do so with humility and with the awareness that we might get it wrong. Hence, we apply that term selectively, not promiscuously. Not every Christian male from the past is considered a Father of the church. There are difficult cases, but let's begin with some uncontroversial figures.

There is no serious dispute about the sanctity of Anthony the Great; Maximus the Confessor's holiness is also uncontested;

Athanasius ran into trouble pretty much constantly during his lifetime, but his posthumous reputation is solid; even to raise the question with respect to the Mother of God smacks of blasphemy or, what is worse, stupid provocation. Conversely, Judas Iscariot is an object of horror and revulsion, notwithstanding the reputation he seems to have enjoyed in whatever circles gave rise to an ancient Coptic *Gospel of Judas* (recently translated and published); Arius is beyond the pale; likewise, Apollinaris, Heracleon, Hierax, and Montanus (whose names become obscure, for good reason). There is also middle ground, in which we encounter the names of influential but sometimes contentious figures like Origen of Alexandria, Gregory of Nyssa, and Augustine of Hippo. For the moment what matters is that we have a good sense for putting other people either to the left or to the right of the group of the Fathers.

An example taken from the contemporary academic study of ancient Christianity helps clarify what is at stake in the business of selecting some people and affiliating ourselves to them. Every four years the University of Oxford hosts an International Conference on Patristic Study. These conferences are a major event in the scholarly community and have been so for over half a century. As such, they are an important indicator of trends in how the term "patristics" is used and understood. Classical disciplines in studying the church fathers are regularly on display at the conference, such as the history of dogma, the publication of critical editions of ancient Christian documents, and the theological exposition of patristic literature. What someone outside the academic guild might not expect is how accommodating the modern study of "patristics" can be. The Oxford Conference is a venue for modes of study which can also be conspicuously hostile to theology, or devoted to interpreting ancient documents with reference to the latest trends in literary theory, or focused solely on the social history of ancient Christianity (perhaps in comparison with other religions from that era).

More important for our purposes, patristic studies can also incorporate the serious, sympathetic study of heresy and heretics on their own terms. In the published acts from these conferences, *Studia Patristica,* this fact has often been obscured by the coy subtitles under which papers are organized, such as *Athanasius and His Opponents* and *Other Latin Writers.* The word "patristic" in contemporary academia has thus become detached from the theologically informed reference to the church fathers (which I have been advocating as its primary sense) and has been applied instead to a particular historical epoch during which certain people lived. Since this terminological shift has in fact occurred in the scholarly conversation, there is no obvious way to deny admission to a conference on "patristics" to the sympathetic study of ancient heretics. And yet, there is a tremendous difference between thinking that "patristic" refers to a by-gone era of political and cultural transformation in the post-classical Mediterranean world, on the one hand, and thinking that it evokes a network of claims about theology in historical perspective, on the other. To be sure, theologians are by no means excluded from the undertaking: the theological study of early Christianity is still an authentic enterprise, albeit one that may seem a little staid and boring alongside the other methodologies that are proliferating so exuberantly.

The scholar Patrick Henry gave a shrewd evaluation of this process in a communication delivered in Oxford about a quarter of a century ago, under the telling title: "Why Is Contemporary

Scholarship So Enamored of Ancient Heresies?"[1] Henry identified several factors that dispose many modern scholars kindly toward ancient heresies. He singled out for attention a tendency to interpret all things politically, an entrenched cynicism toward political power, a deep sympathy for the politically disenfranchised, and in the final analysis a habit of identifying heresy as an expression of political protest and thus heretics as sympathetic underdogs. (He wasn't imagining those trends, and they weren't new. They had been noted and criticized, for other reasons, by A.H.M. Jones in an important article which posed the question, "Were ancient heresies national or social movements in disguise?")[2] The configuration of ideas described by Henry is problematic because it subsumes all aspects of life and thought under politics. For this reason, the exercise of political power comes to be taken as the "real meaning" of Christian debate in the late ancient world. And so theology is readily subordinated to politics in such interpretations of the beliefs of early Christians.

These developments make it urgent for theologians who are committed to patristic theology to think thoroughly and clearly about what distinguishes Fathers from other ancient Christian writers, and both groups from heretics. As children of the Fathers of the Church, we affiliate with certain saints as parental figures. Which ones? And why? Given the trend of recent scholarship, we need to be able to explain *why* is it that we consider Athanasius of Alexandria a Father, Lactantius simply an ancient Christian writer, and Arius a heretic. This is an *apologetic* need in a pecu-

[1] Patrick Henry, "Why Is Contemporary Scholarship So Enamored of Ancient Heresies?" *Studia Patristica* 17 (1980): 123–26.

[2] A.H.M. Jones, "Were Ancient Heresies National or Social Movements in Disguise?" *Journal of Theological Studies* n.s. 10 (1959): 280–98.

liar sense of that word that will be familiar to those who have read the defenses of Christianity by Justin Martyr or Irenaeus of Lyons (or, for that matter, Plato's *Apology of Socrates*)—a need, that is, to be able to offer a reasoned explanation for the sake of defending oneself from misunderstanding or misrepresentation. An explanation of this sort is just what we require if we want to insist that the term "patristic" implies a family relationship that is ongoing, in contrast to the idea that it merely refers to an era in the distant past that falls between classical antiquity and the early middle ages. Such an explanation will have the added benefit of enabling us to reject the idea that the history of Christian doctrine is merely an account of ideological and political victories that, in turn, redefine subsequent understanding of earlier events. An explanation of this kind clarifies how patristic theology is a record of the continuing process of reflecting upon the revelation of God in Jesus Christ.

There is a clear alternative to developing an apologetic along the lines I have just sketched. It begins with accepting the reputation that we as Orthodox enjoy (and sometimes cultivate) for unrivalled continuity with the Christian past. On the basis of that reputation, one could assert that being Orthodox leads to a privileged understanding of the ancient church and that this understanding is preferable to the results of academic study. This option has the satisfying outcome of securing the theological study of patristic sources. But it does so at a cost. The security it provides is the security of a ghetto. It also increases the likelihood of confusing prejudices with insights. Above all, it betrays our responsibility to bear witness to Christ. Simply talking amongst ourselves is not a legitimate option.

The changes in scholarship surveyed above have been going on for long enough that their consequences are felt publicly. In order to bear witness to Christ in today's world, this fact cannot be ignored. As evidence, I appeal to the experience of looking through the religion section in bookshops, where specialist monographs on late antiquity are shelved alongside books on theology. People could be excused for supposing, wrongly, that the great historian Peter Brown is a theologian. In any case, the public impact of patristic studies obliges us to think about how we relate to the people whom we are happy to call our Fathers. By dwelling on the different current uses of the term "patristic," we have seen that there are important implications. When we use the terms "patristic" and "fathers," we are not referring simply to a remote period in the past; nor do we apply it indiscriminately to people who lived in the past. Instead, those terms are used selectively. We are collectively looking back and acknowledging our debts to certain people who have gone on before. Very frequently, we then address ourselves to them seeking their intercession before God on our behalf, thus asserting that we and they belong to a coherent community. It is only a slight overstatement to say that, when we refer to some people (but not others) as Fathers, what happens is that *we* identify *them* as standing in a parental relationship to us. We are, if you like, adopting them as our parents. This family relationship, like all relationships, is dynamic. We will get a better idea of the dynamics at work in our affiliation to them by considering the legacy of Orthodoxy, which pervades and sustains that relationship.

## The Heritage

We turn now to heritage, the second major theme of this chapter. It seems good to begin with a familiar word that recurs frequently in conversations of all sorts about Orthodoxy: "tradition." One typical refrain in conversations about "tradition" is the distinction between "the tradition" and "traditions,"[3] or more colloquially "big-T Tradition" and "little-t traditions." That distinction has proved helpful to many who come into Orthodoxy from a Protestant background, who have a strongly adverse reaction to the "traditions of men," which they take as the point of the episode in St Mark's Gospel in which the Pharisees confront Christ about the disciples' failure to wash their hands before eating. It will be useful at this point, not least in thinking about how complicated and ambiguous that passage from the Bible is, to reflect on the difference between "Tradition"—which is permanent—and "traditions"—which are negotiable.

Christ does not categorically oppose "the commandment of God" to the "traditions of men"; instead, he castigates the Pharisees for holding to tradition in a way that amounts to "laying aside" or even "rejecting" God's commandment and "making the word of God of no effect" (see Mk 7.6–13). The problem is when "traditions" clash with God's commandments, but this does not mean that "traditions" are intrinsically bad. In fact, other passages clearly indicate otherwise. The Thessalonians are bidden "stand fast, and hold the traditions which ye have been taught, whether by word, or our epistle" (2 Thess 2.15; see also 2 Thess 3.6). The apostolic tradition, so far from making the word of God

[3]See Yves Congar, OP, *The Meaning of Tradition* (San Francisco: Ignatius Press, 2004); Vladimir Lossky, *The Mystical Theology of the Eastern Church* (Crestwood, NY: St Vladimir's Seminary Press, 1976), esp. pp. 7–22.

ineffectual, serves precisely to encourage us to enact it. Or, to return to those colloquial terms, the "little-t traditions" serve to promote the "big-T Tradition." Naturally, they are subordinated to them, and over time they may well change or be altered to make them more effective in promoting "big-T Tradition."

The difference in principle is clear: whatever is part of the "big-T Tradition" is a non-negotiable feature of Orthodox Christianity. "Big-T Tradition" is that without which Orthodoxy does not exist. "Little-t traditions," on the other hand, are second-level features of Orthodoxy. This does not make them dispensable, and it does not trivialize them. They are recognizable characteristics of the expression of Orthodoxy. The distinction helps us see how not all particular features of the expression of Orthodoxy in one culture or one time are obligatory for all Orthodox Christians at all times and everywhere. There is an old motto that neatly expresses the point: "Unity in essentials, variety in non-essentials, and charity in all things."

Some of the best examples come from variation in liturgical practice, which are familiar to anyone who has worshipped in different churches. The fact that a priest might recite some liturgical prayers under his breath, or might say them out loud, is a case in point. Exactly how those prayers are recited is less important than that they are recited, and neither practice compromises Orthodoxy. Or consider the variation within prayerbooks. The same prayers are repeated, usually in the same order, but the translations vary—sometimes dramatically. This is not to deny that there are standards to evaluate the translations (or the liturgical practices), but merely to point out that a more or less substantial amount of variation is acceptable as a matter of course. Whenever we accept the legitimacy of variations in practice (as we often do), we are already implicitly acknowledging a difference between "the Tradition" and "traditions."

## The Neo-Patristic Synthesis

Living in accordance with tradition has been a stable feature of Orthodox Christianity since time out of memory. In recent times *tradition* itself has become an object of attention. Tradition is one of the main features in an exceptionally vital movement within Orthodoxy. I am referring to the neo-patristic synthesis. This movement was advanced especially by the numerous writings of Fr Georges Florovsky (1893–1979), who in addition to being an influential theologian was also a respected church historian. In the process of critically studying the history of Russian theology, a process that resulted in his massive *Ways of Russian Theology*, Florovsky noted that centuries ago a breach had opened up in Orthodoxy between theology and the ecclesiastical experience of prayer, which resulted in a rupture between intellect and instinct. The experience of this rupture was felt by many intelligent and devout people, who responded with an almost frenetic level of social and ecclesiastical activity and an astounding outpouring of writings in the nineteenth century.

Unfortunately, according to Florovsky, most of the responses served only to compound the problem. Some of the responses introduced alien habits of thought into Russian Orthodoxy and thus generated *pseudomorphoses* ("false forms") of Orthodoxy. Some of them cultivated a false nostalgia that in turn contributes to sectarianism and hostility. Some of them even encouraged what he memorably called "an exodus from history" through insisting, occasionally quite forcefully, on separating themselves and their Christian outlook (in some cases, their Church) from the traditional Byzantine Greek heritage of Russian Orthodoxy.

As a deliberate contrast to the responses of the nineteenth century, Florovsky based his Christian reply to the crisis of modern life on a conscientious entry into the historical experience of Christianity in all its details and particulars, including first and foremost the experience of Christian worship. It is significant that Florovsky considered the liturgical books of the Church to have been the first theological texts he read. Because he identified the breach between theology and prayer as the underlying cause of the problem, he advocated the integration of worship and understanding in the classical Byzantine mode—with all that implies, not least in terms of self-discipline, charity, and ascetic humility—as the only way forward for a meaningful contemporary theology. His solution to the problems of modern Christian life was the call for a creative appropriation of historical Christian belief. Florovsky believed and argued that such a solution is relevant not only to the Orthodox, but to the Christian world at large, since the problems are common to us all. By no means were Russians alone in experiencing the effects of a "dissociation of sensibility," to borrow a phrase that T.S. Eliot memorably used when he was analyzing comparable trends in the literature of the seventeenth century.

Florovsky's extensive work with the World Council of Churches in its early days was in large measure an attempt to make the results of his distinctly Orthodox project available to all sympathetic Christians. He did not conceive of the project as a justification for retrograde nationalism, mechanical repetitiveness, or saccharine nostalgia. It was to be an intense and intensive recourse to tradition that would be much more than an exercise in antiquarianism. Florovsky described his project this way:

> [it] should be more than just a collection of Patristic sayings or statements. It must be a *synthesis*, a creative reassessment of those insights which were granted to the Holy Men of old. It must be *Patristic*, faithful to the spirit and vision of the Fathers, *ad mentem Patrum*. Yet, it must also be *Neo-Patristic*, since it is to be addressed to the new age, with its own problems and queries.[4]

The synthesis thus conceived is necessarily a dynamic engagement with the modern world. Florovsky's vision of theology is broad and generous enough (and his understanding of the history of Orthodox theology critical enough) to enable him to take very seriously the proposition that the Orthodox can and should learn from other Christians. His vision of Orthodox theology also incorporates a call for seriousness, even professionalism, with respect to the historical sources.

Through the forceful critiques advanced in his *Ways of Russian Theology*, Florovsky created a space in which the neo-patristic synthesis could function. First, he criticized the attempt to redress Orthodox problems through a syncretistic approach to religious experience, as illustrated, for example, in the writings of the visionary religious philosopher Vladimir Soloviev. Florovsky also expressed dismay at the presumption that tradition is some sort of automatic and inerrant vehicle by which Orthodoxy perennially renews and perpetuates itself. Hence, his great insistence

---

[4]This lecture is related by Andrew Blane, *Georges Florovsky: Russian Intellectual, Orthodox Churchman* (Crestwood, NY: St Vladimir's Seminary Press, 1993), pp. 153–55 at 154.

on the ascetic effort—his word is *podvig*—that is required of us in maintaining and cultivating Orthodox tradition. According to its principal architect, the neo-patristic synthesis is not a sterile recapitulation of age-old truths. It is rather an honest engagement with the present informed by an awareness of the past that is critical, scrupulous, and honest.

## Russian Religious Philosophy

Recent years have seen a proliferation of studies dedicated to alternative (and in some cases competing) schools in contemporary Orthodox Christianity. There is a regular cottage industry of publishing now on various aspects of the writings and thought of Fr Sergius Bulgakov, for example, which have argued with conviction that he should be taken seriously as a major modern Orthodox theologian. Without commenting on the merits or demerits of that scholarly trend, it is entirely appropriate for us to question the tendency in some recent books to contrast the neo-patristic synthesis and Russian philosophical theology as starkly as possible.

As a case in point, we can turn to Paul Valliere's fascinating *Modern Russian Theology*. In commending the Russian school as one of the "principled alternatives in Orthodox theology"[5] to the neo-patristic synthesis that deserves serious consideration, he makes a series of positive statements about Russian philosophical theology as practiced by Soloviev and others and interweaves them with a fairly unflattering assessment of neo-patristic Orthodox theology. Valliere considers neo-patristic theology so dominant in

---

[5]P. Valliere, *Modern Russian Theology: Bukharev, Soloviev, Bulgakov: Orthodox Theology in a New Key* (Edinburgh: T & T Clark, 2000), p. 6.

Orthodoxy that it lacks internal criticism, that it fails to provide theological guidance to contemporary problems that are political and social in character, and by implication, that it fails to speak theologically to Orthodoxy's relation to the modern world.[6] He returns with gusto to these themes in the final chapter of his book.

That chapter, called "The Limits of Tradition," traces the ascendancy of neo-patristic scholarship as against Russian philosophical theology. No doubt, Valliere's account is sometimes painfully accurate, as when he comments on the contraction of Orthodox theology into an exercise in expositing a narrow selection of ancient writings on key themes. He takes particular issue with formulations of the scope of the neo-patristic synthesis by Fr Alexander Schmemann, Fr John Meyendorff, and Fr Thomas Hopko, in which "the concept of tradition is not just one of a number of formative or organizing concepts in Neopatristic theology, but the hegemonic concept, the central idea, the practical absolute."[7] This is not the place to adjudicate between Valliere on the one hand and the three former deans of St Vladimir's Seminary on the other. Valliere certainly makes a forceful point, but his estimation of the relevance, or otherwise, of the neo-patristic synthesis and the resources it brings to contemporary theology is prone to exaggeration.

Valliere contrasts two possibilities—either "beyond the fathers" or "back to the fathers"—and indicates that the former represents the typical attitude of the Russian school of philosophical theology, and the latter represents the typical attitude in the neo-patristic

[6]Ibid., pp. 6–7.

[7]Ibid., p. 377.

synthesis. I want to explore this characterization because, even though I disagree with some points that Valliere makes on its basis, the contrast is valuable for refining our understanding of how we should engage with the past.

Going "beyond the fathers" seems to suggest that the spirit of the philosophical theologians and authors of twentieth-century Russia was transgressive, and perhaps amongst some it was. Even so, it is striking that Valliere's representatives of this movement, Alexander Bukharev, Sergius Bulgakov, and Vladimir Soloviev, remained Orthodox. (I am assuming this is true of Soloviev, despite some reports that he died a Catholic.) This means that the subjects of his book were members of a subset within a larger group of thinkers, poets, and visionaries. Their imaginative power and creative genius makes them comparable to some of their contemporaries, whose perspectives on Christianity were far more adventurous and took them quite a bit further "beyond the fathers" than, say, Soloviev managed to go. Let's take D. S. Merezhkovsky for an example. He was certainly a Russian religious thinker and his *Jesus the Unknown* assuredly goes "beyond the fathers." If we take a view of Russian religious philosophy broad enough to include him, then what we see is that Bukharev, Soloviev, Florensky, Bulgakov, Berdiaev, and others actually didn't go nearly as far as they might have done.

As for the possibility of going "back to the fathers," a letter written by Gilbert Burnet, bishop of Salisbury, on April 5, 1698, provides us with a fairly good specimen of what that entails. Commenting on Peter the Great's travels in Britain, the bishop observed that "the Czar's priest is come over, who is truly a holy man, and more learned than I could have imagined, but thinks it a great piece of religion to be no wiser than his fathers, and therefore cannot bear the thought of imagining that anything among them can want amendment."[8] Popular resistance to change, verging on atavism, is similarly found in a response written to Pope Pius IX's encyclical "Ad Orientales" (January 6, 1848). The patriarchs of the four Eastern Orthodox sees and members of their holy synods gave this account of the bulwark that protects the Orthodox faith: "Moreover, neither patriarchs nor councils could then have introduced novelties amongst us, because the protector of religion is the very body of the church, even the people themselves, *who desire their religious worship to be ever unchanged and of the same kind as that of their fathers.*"[9] Further evidence of this mindset could be provided, and it would only bolster the intuitive appeal, basic to Valliere's contrast, that going "back to the fathers" is a retrograde, if not counter-revolutionary, thing to do.

The problem is that, according to Florovsky's description of the program, the neo-patristic synthesis differs from both of Valliere's categories in a fundamental way. Florovsky's project was a creative reassessment of the insights of the Fathers that is addressed to the problems and queries of the modern age. In the neo-patristic mode of theology, going back to the Fathers is not an end unto itself. Nor does the theological exposition of their

---

[8] See James Cracraft, *The Church Reform of Peter the Great* (Stanford, CA: Stanford University Press, 1971), pp. 33–34.

[9] *Response to Pope Pius IX* §17, emphasis added; trans. J. Pelikan and V. Hotchkiss, *Creeds and Confessions of Faith in the Christian Tradition, III: Modern Christianity* (New Haven, CT: Yale University Press, 2003), pp. 265–88 at 282. I have followed here the title given by Pelikan and Hotchkiss, but the document is known more widely as the *Encyclical of the Eastern Patriarchs.*

writings exhaust the purpose of neo-patristic theology. The first move in the neo-patristic synthesis is indeed "back to the fathers," but if it is the final move, it would be a poor synthesis. Instead, it be a "neo-patristic repetition" (or not "neo-" at all), which in some regrettable cases is exactly what it is (and here Valliere's criticism is pertinent). Precisely as a synthesis, Florovsky's project involves a second movement from the historical survey to the contemporary situation.

Valliere's contrast—between going "back to the fathers" and going "beyond them"—is questionable. First, as Valliere himself shows at some length, theologians in the Russian philosophical school saw themselves as building on patristic foundations. An extremely important critical evaluation of patristic theology by a leading philosophical theologian—Bulgakov's "Dogma and dogmatics"—makes the point clearly.[10] Second, what Valliere deplores seems to be going back to the fathers *and staying there,* and he is undoubtedly right to critique that practice. However, that is not the agenda of the neo-patristic synthesis. Even in cases where contemporary neo-patristic Orthodox theology seems to be in danger of restricting itself to the historical and theological exposition of ancient classics, we are able to identify the problem and its solution simply by implementing the actual principles that Florovsky outlined. In other words, what Valliere is rightly criticizing is an avoidable failure and not a systemic problem. We go *back to the fathers* in order to move *forward with the fathers*—but not forward *from* the fathers (leaving them behind).

[10]See Peter Bouteneff, trans. "Dogma and Dogmatic Theology," in Michael Plekon, ed., *Tradition Alive: On the Church and the Christian Life in Our Time* (Sheed & Ward/Rowman & Littlefield, 2003), pp. 67–80.

I have questioned the contrast Valliere proposed, but taking his criticism seriously has helped clarify a significant point. Going to the fathers is not an abandonment of the present. It is entirely possible (even necessary) to expect theologians to provide more than antiques. Theology is not authenticated by its use of ancient technical language, and an over-preoccupation with the past is frequently morbid and problematic. But, as I have suggested, these observations are not foreign to the neo-patristic synthesis.

## "Living Tradition"

To convey the connection that links us to the ancients, the expression "living tradition" is often used. Valliere offers a critique of this expression. Here, too, his comments help bring into focus the relationship between tradition and faith. He encourages us to think more deeply about the nature of history.

Valliere finds the idea of "living tradition" to be problematic, contending that it conflates things that can be handed down with things that cannot be handed down. He notes first that if something is *traditional* then it must be involved in a process of transmission over time.[11] Next, he gives good reasons to be worried by claims that the content of living tradition is Christ Himself. Such claims would appear to treat the Living Christ as though he himself were being transmitted from one generation to the next, seemingly reducing Christ from a person to a thing. Indeed, this is deeply troubling. Further, to say that Christ is the *content* of tradition is to imply that tradition *contains* Christ, and that implication is wholly objectionable. (Much better, if less elegant

[11]Valliere, *Modern Russian Theology*, pp. 379–80.

in plain English, is to say that Christ is the *referent* of tradition and that tradition *refers to* Christ.)

Valliere next brings faith into the analysis. He argues that the problem of faith shows up another serious shortcoming in the neo-patristic attitude toward the past. Florovsky's argument about the foundational importance of history for theology, writes Valliere,

> underemphasizes, indeed overlooks, the very real tension between an appeal to history and an act of faith. An act of faith can only happen "now" as opposed to "then"; it can never be a *traditum*. An act of faith takes place in that mysterious gap between the not-yet-historical and the already-historical where human life is actually lived.[12]

It is reasonable to call attention to Florovsky's remarkable bias toward historical research. Of course, the act of faith "occurs" in the present, not the past. (Presumably other acts of faith "occurred" in the past, or "will occur" in the future.) Valliere's claim becomes more obscure when he invokes a "mysterious gap" and refers to the "not-yet-historical." The use of these terms conjures up shades of Martin Heidegger and suggests that Valliere is concerned with an abstract, but crucial, metaphysical proposition about time.

Let's return to the metaphysics of time and faith after we have addressed a more urgent concern. Valliere asserts that an act of faith "can never be a *traditum*"—that is, it can never be the thing *handed down*. That assertion rests on a number of beliefs about the character of faith and its origins. We need to tease them out. As we do so, we will be simultaneously building up a case for preferring the term "heritage" to the term "tradition."

[12]Ibid., p. 382.

* * *

Let's start with the words "act of faith." This expression is ambiguous: it might mean "faith enacted" or else it might mean "faith as an act" (*faithing*, so to speak). The first possibility would mean the active expression of faith. The second possibility would emphasize that faith itself is the very act of responding to the message (or the person) of Jesus Christ. Now the second possibility requires something more sophisticated than the first. For one thing, it requires us to understand "faith" as a verb. What might "to faith" mean? There is nothing in Valliere's criticism that makes it necessary to attribute to him this more complicated sense of the expression. It seems, then, that he is emphasizing that faith is *active* and not claiming that faith is an action. Any faith worthy of the name will find its expression in the actions of the faithful. Faith without works is, after all, dead.

If this is right, what we are facing here is a claim about how tradition relates to action. Valliere seems to be distinguishing active faith from tradition, on the basis that tradition is not applicable to action. The extract from his argument quoted above suggests that tradition and enacting faith are distinct because tradition concerns the past and action concerns the present. We need to be mindful about how we proceed from here. For, as the philosopher and archaeologist R. G. Collingwood warned in his book *The Idea of History*, there is a simple misunderstanding involved in supposing that history occurs in the past. According to Collingwood, history is a disciplined activity in terms of which we survey records (including written records, material evidence, oral accounts, and forms of practice, amongst other things) that derive from and/or pertain to events from the past, and then work out an account of the past using them. History is an activity; it is something that we do *in the present* as we survey evidence of the past.

Taking up this observation from Collingwood, we can say that tradition is a disciplined activity in terms of which we survey records (including written records, material evidence, oral accounts, and forms of practice, amongst other things) that derive from and/or pertain to events from the past and work out a strategy of acting in the present. There is nothing in the make-up of tradition that keeps it from being relevant to the present. In fact, quite the opposite: it is precisely determining what from the past *is* relevant to the present that is the domain of tradition. The major function that tradition plays is well described by Florovsky:

> Orthodoxy is not a thing which can be kept simply by inertia. No tradition can survive unless it is continued in a creative effort. The message of Christ is eternal and always the same, but it must be reinterpreted again and again so as to become a challenge to every new generation . . . We have not simply to keep the legacy of the past, we have to do everything we can in order to present it to others as a living thing . . . .[13]

Is Valliere correct in saying that the act of faith occurs not in the past, nor in the future, but in the gap between them (that is, in the present)? We can begin an answer by saying that, so far as we are aware, all events occur in the present. Past events by definition no longer occur; future events by definition cannot have occurred yet and so must be regarded as contingent. The present is the only field of action or field for activity. For this reason, it is not illuminating to insist that an act occurs in the present. But even more importantly, emphatic stress on actions that are happening "now"

[13]See Blane, *Georges Florovsky*, p. 93.

can distract us from actions that began in the past and continue in the present. Those actions bridge the "mysterious gap" between the past and the present. And it seems reasonable to assume that some of them will probably carry forward into the future, too. Memory enables us to work with the building blocks of the past and shape them into a coherent structure for the present. A present coherence, in turn, should serve to achieve a future goal.

A related point about the present understood as a "mysterious gap" can be taken from another of Collingwood's insights. As Collingwood noted, the beginning of history is memory—and from this we get a sense of how contrived it is to insist that the present is a mysterious gap between the already and the not-yet. While I sit here typing, it is memory and the judicious glance back over a few pages that enables me to build up my words into a paragraph that is coherent with what I have already written. After all, I wrote the beginning of this paragraph some time ago, not now. The act of writing this chapter began in the past, it is what I am doing right now, and it will have to continue into the future if I am to bring the chapter to a close. So this very act of writing has a "historical" component. By the same token, an act of faith may occur "now," but this does not preclude a historical component to the act of faith.

There is another odd thing in the way Valliere contrasts faith to history. It is revealed by his criticism of the (admittedly overused) expression "living tradition," where he writes that

> A living thing, *qua* living thing, cannot be a tradition, for its life is immanent, its own, not received from others. [ . . . ] That which is handed down is by definition a *traditum,* and even the action of handing down can be viewed as a tradition

to the extent that it follows an antecedent pattern (which it almost always does). But the act itself, because it issues from someone's free decision, is new every time it is performed. An a-traditional and un-traditionalizable element—the "living" element—has entered in.[14]

The striking thing in this criticism is its supposition that a "living thing, *qua* living thing, cannot be a tradition, for its life is immanent, its own, not received from others" and the related idea that "the act itself, because it issues from someone's free decision, is new every time it is performed." According to this critique of tradition, the characteristics of a "living" thing are that its vitality is immanent (rather than derivative) and that its origin is voluntaristic, i.e. that it issues from the free decision of a personal agent. Furthermore, these are precisely the features of a "living" thing that, we are told, make it "a-traditional and un-traditionalizable." The proposed contrast between a living thing and a *traditum* is extremely vivid—but it is not clear that we need to accept it.

What happens if we apply these characterizations to the activity of a "living faith"? Under these conditions, for faith to be living and active, that which makes it living must be "immanent, its own, and not received from others." But this is wrong. Life itself is received from others. Indeed *everything* is received from others—for "What have you that you did not receive? If then you received it, why do you boast as if it were not a gift?" (1 Cor 4.7) Are we so self-sufficient and independent that, for something to be properly our own, it must originate from the inner depths of our individuality, and it must be ours and ours alone? Faith is not exclusively personal. It is shared and inherently communal.

[14]Valliere, *Modern Russian Theology*, p. 383.

We receive faith in two ways. First, we learn faith. We are concerned here with active, living faith; how do we learn to live and act faithfully? We learn how to act not through the free self-expression of an inscrutable inward agency that has spontaneously decided to act, but by observing and imitating the actions of others who already know how to act. These other people might teach us actively or passively, by modeling a particular kind of action. Similarly, learning faith follows from "being begotten in faith." We have both instructors in Christ, who teach us the faith, and fathers in Christ who beget us through the gospel (see 1 Cor 4.15). In all of these examples, to enact faith is by no means antithetical to tradition. While it would be imprecise and misleading to say that faith *is* tradition, we should say that living faith can be *traditional*. Tradition itself is not an external, mechanical force to be contrasted to an internal dynamism.

* * *

There is a tangle of problems related to the use, misuse, and abuse of tradition in Christian theology. This tangle has grown impressively in the early modern era in the wake of polemics between different Christian confessions. However, the fact that a term can be misunderstood is not an adequate reason for abandoning it. What needs to be done is to clarify its meaning, and this we have done in response to Valliere's numerous criticisms against the "traditionalism" of the neo-patristic synthesis. I have argued against several of his specific claims, but I have generally agreed with his diagnosis that the word "tradition" suggests an emphasis on the past, and how we regard the past is a contested subject. Without disavowing the word "tradition," it will be helpful to complement it by using another term that, while not being entirely synonymous, significantly overlaps the semantic domain of "tradition" without evoking age-old problems. The term I have chosen for present purposes is *heritage.*

Like "tradition," the word "heritage" immediately evokes the idea of passing on something: an inheritance. Just as the *traditum* is only one element within a tradition, likewise the inheritance is only one element within a heritage. In both cases, there is also the process of transmission to be considered. In neither case is the emphasis limited to things past. We are also talking about an activity by means of which something from the past is retained in the present. A heritage is not inherited until it is taken up; a tradition is not traditional until it is enacted. Likewise, in both cases, what is handed on is not limited to a physical thing. A tradition or a heritage can refer to an entire manner of living, a whole culture.

But there is also an intuitive difference between the two concepts that serves my purposes very well. Whereas "tradition" suggests an emphasis on something from the past being handed down, "heritage" suggests an emphasis on something from the past being received—and, even more significantly, something in the present that can become again the inheritance of another, younger generation. It is more difficult, given the available language, to talk about the future in terms of tradition. But it is easily possible to talk about the future in terms of heritage. An old saying, popularly attributed to Native American wisdom, makes the point neatly: we do not (merely) inherit the earth from our parents; we hold it in trust for our children. An inheritance is something that is received and then transmitted to heirs—ideally, after it has been increased through responsible stewardship. The language of heritage has a range that is greater in useful ways than the language of tradition.

———

Earlier in this chapter, we briefly considered our utter and entire dependence upon God as it is reflected in the numerous ways in which we are similarly dependent upon our parents. I suggested that society is an extension of a network of relations upon which we are dependent. The concept of inheritance demonstrates its worth in this context. Society is more than a group of interlinking familial and social connections. It is also made up of the ways of behaving and understanding that support those connections. Culture is inherited and transmitted within complex, overlapping, and communicating social networks. Like any other inheritance, it is something that we receive and accept (we don't simply pull it out of thin air or, even worse, out of old books). But again like any other inheritance it is also something that we increase and protect so that we ourselves can in good time bequeath it to our own heirs.

Our heritage in the Church is not restricted to the lofty heights of doctrine or the ornate intricacy of Byzantine chant. It is not limited to writings or buildings. It is pervasive. It tutors us in appropriate behavior. It colors the very words that we use. In a powerful section from his excellent book *The Dominion of the Dead*, Robert Pogue Harrison comments on the fact that we speak the words of the dead. Our language reverberates down the centuries, being enriched (or impoverished, sometimes) through its usage. The vocabulary of daily speech has been used before and the words have acquired connotation through that usage. The word "rose" is a good example: "a rose is a rose . . . ," "a rose by any other name . . . ," "rosy dawn," "every rose has its thorn," and so on and so forth. With respect to our Orthodox heritage, words in common usage take on particular colorations: think of "icon," "baptism," and "creed." If you are an Orthodox

Christian, you probably were thinking of a Byzantine representation of Jesus Christ or a saint, and *not* a point-and-click link on your computer's display; or of a three-fold emersion into a font, and *not* pouring water over a baby's forehead; and the Nicene-Constantinopolitan Creed, but definitely *not* with the clause that the Spirit proceeds from the Son as well as the Father. Language as a whole carries a jumble of associations. The use of the words of previous generations (or, in Robert Pogue Harrison's formula, of the dead) means that their experience becomes a constant feature of how we perceive life and how we act upon our perceptions.

The process of transmission is not tidy. If we wish, we can identify various false starts and dead ends and even moribund habits. But we can also find examples of startling insight, courageous fidelity, and exceptional vitality. These are the elements of human experience over time. Over time, inevitably, inescapably, change occurs. Such is life, and in itself change is neither good nor bad. Our criteria for discerning the good from the bad have to do not solely with pedigree and antiquity, but with the love and peace of God, which are neither abstract ideas nor evanescent feelings. They are not isolated from the collective experience and conversation of the people. It is precisely through entering into collective experience and conversation that we recognize and promote godliness in our lives, our families, our societies.

As far as we can tell, this dynamic has constantly been active. Emphases vary down the centuries, practices evolve, attitudes change. But the process itself—the process of sharing life by entering into a multitude of relationships—is stable in the way only a dynamic thing can be stable. To look back for a moment at

Valliere's concerns about tradition, what we can see is that his case is initially appealing only because he contrasts the patristic era with the modern era in a way that implies the radical discontinuity between the two, and thus the irrelevance of the former for the latter. Hence, his provocative claim that the resources of the neo-patristic synthesis are inadequate to responding to contemporary economic, social, and environmental problems. The resources are inadequate, on Valliere's line, because they are drawn from the ancient world and nothing in antiquity corresponds to modern problems. There is a badness of fit.

Valliere's claim has some appeal if we suppose that all good theology is a recapitulation of ancient theology, that everything of theological value has already been said and all we need to do is update the language in which it is expressed. But why would we think that? It is precisely when we fail to recognize that the heritage that comes down to us from that era *is* constantly refreshed and modified—when we fail to see that it is very much a going concern—that we are beguiled into thinking that the world of the ancients is discontinuous with ours. It is an easy mistake to make, particularly since there is a widespread tendency to think of the Christian east as somehow being timeless. But that is confusion: the Christian east has had a different historical experience than the Christian west has had, but that does not mean that God has somehow preserved it, changeless, as the centuries rolled on. A different historical experience is not the same thing as an experience that is not historical at all.

The Orthodox Church is not mysteriously exempt from the challenge of time. Instead, the Church has the promise of her Lord that the Holy Spirit will abide with her, and it is precisely this abiding presence that makes for *spiritual* fathers and mothers, who are thus a permanent feature of the Church. For the sake of conceptual clarity, we can make an artificial distinction as a brief experiment: let's use the term "patristic" to describe the age of the ancient Fathers of the church, to about A.D. 800; the term "Church Fathers," on the other hand, will refer to those men and women who exemplify the effects of the abiding presence of the Holy Spirit within the church, without limitation to a particular age or era. They are the spiritual fathers and mothers of the Church throughout its long and often tumultuous history. The "patristic" Fathers (a cumbersome and redundant expression, I know) are the spiritual Fathers of the Church in antiquity. They lived during the long dusk of the Roman Empire, true, but what makes them Fathers is that they lived in the presence of God. In these terms, the neo-patristic synthesis is less about the re-appropriation across the centuries of the "patristic Fathers" than it is about the appropriation of the "mind of the Fathers" (or, to use Florovsky's gloss, their "spirit and vision"), which has never been extinguished. Because there is no loss of continuity in the Spirit's presence within the church, it is meaningless to talk as though the Fathers are restricted to any given historical era.

The awareness that there is no historical discontinuity means that when we say we "adopt" the Fathers, we need to be clear that this act doesn't occur across a historical chasm. We aren't cherry-picking the best and brightest that remote history has to offer. If we were simply identifying favored people who lived a thousand years ago or more, and claiming an affinity to them, that alone would be reason enough to suspect that something arbitrary was happening. But since God's people are renewed day by day in every successive generation, and since we recognize and celebrate the saints' holiness (which in reality is nothing other than God's holiness in their lives), when we find it in our contemporaries, that worry is allayed. There is a continuous and cumulative practice of identifying God's love and life as expressed in all human beings ancient and modern. We do not make an imaginative leap into the great unknown. Rather, within an ongoing historical succession, we are referred to exemplars of conspicuous holiness across the entire history of the Church. This process has been going on for so long already that it has an important history of its own. The next chapter will give us an opportunity to look more closely into this process of transmission and appropriation.

* * *

Some people might find the idea that we move about in an environment thoroughly saturated by history and tradition to be threatening. It may seem to reduce the possibility of free action. Such concerns are understandable, because freedom is valued extremely highly in post-industrialized societies. But freedom is far more impaired when we are naïve about the conditions in which it is possible to act freely. To understand the dense connections, the historical continuations, the momentum of events, and to weigh these factors in one's considerations, is foundational to acting freely. To neglect them is to abridge one's freedom. Ignorance is not conducive to freedom, and knowledge is not injurious to responsibility. We understand our present situation better when we are aware of the factors that contributed to it.

It is far more common these days to want to look ahead than it is to look behind. One of the greatest overarching themes that modern people use to make sense of their lives—a modern "myth," if you will—is *progress*. Progress is widely assumed to be a good thing, without further comment. We like to think of ourselves boldly facing a future that we are (at least to some extent) shaping. Since the age of industrialization, the idea that we create our future has been cherished. (It seems fairly obvious, for instance, that many modern problems in bioethics result from applying the ideal of industrialized progress to ourselves.) And if we are going to create the future, we obviously need to orient ourselves toward future goals.

But this is only part of the way we live as humans, and there is an equally important part that is often lost sight of. As important as goal-directed behavior and responsibility are, we are in a very basic sense actually oriented toward the past. We travel through time backward, like Walter Benjamin's "Angel of Progress." Reacting to Paul Klee's painting "Angelus Novus," Benjamin described how fierce winds blowing out of paradise are blasting the angel into an unseen future.[15] There is a neat paraphrase of Benjamin's thesis by Laurie Anderson in her song "The Dream Before": history is an angel being blown backward into the future. Much has been made over the significance of the angel in Benjamin's thinking as a Marxist, a secular Jewish critic, and an essayist,[16] and we don't need to embrace his ideas in order to appreciate the image.

A more prosaic image makes the same point. Consider the rower. It is far easier for us to have a clear idea of where we have just been than it is to have an idea of where we will go next. We might

[15]Walter Benjamin, "On the Concept of History," trans. Harry Zohn, *Walter Benjamin, Selected Writings*, Vol. 4: 1938–1940 (Cambridge, MA: Harvard University Press, 2003), pp. 392–93.

[16]See, for instance, Gershom Scholem, "Walter Benjamin and His Angel," in Gary Smith, ed., *On Walter Benjamin: Critical Essays and Recollections* (Cambridge, MA: MIT Press, 1991), pp. 51–89.

crane our necks around slightly to make out something of what is just about to happen—but in fact we do not stare into the future in the way that common sense suggests. The fact that we are moving backward into the future is why predicting the future is so notoriously difficult. Experience teaches us that predicting beyond a very limited range is unlikely to foretell accurately what will happen. At the same time, it is difficult to see accurately very far into the past.

These limitations should not cause us anxiety or despair. We are not on our own. We are part of a great company that draws on centuries of experience and, unworthy as we are, we enjoy the benevolent presence of the same God who has rejoiced in the company of the saints from the beginning.

*chapter two*

# HOW IS IT TRANSMITTED?

In the first chapter, we reflected on the patristic heritage with reference to the questions of what it means to acknowledge some people as our parents in the faith and what it is that we inherit from them. We noted in particular that, despite some claims to the contrary, we are by no means separated from the ancient Fathers of the Church by a chasm that can only be bridged by a mystical leap of faith. We are all joined together into the Church by God, and we contribute to the Church through participating in a continuous process of inheritance that runs down the ages without interruption. But simply because this process has continued without interruption does not mean that the inheritance itself remains frozen. Taking part in the heritage of the fathers does not protect us from the passage of time and everything that happens in its wake. Actually, thinking of our relationship to patristic theology in terms of a heritage induces us to think about the transmission, propagation, and transformation of the inheritance itself.

In this chapter, we will move from general considerations to some case studies that illustrate the ways in which the patristic heritage is transmitted. To call them "case studies" is to indicate that we will be using modern scholarly techniques to interpret how ancient theology was received in antiquity: how did the fathers receive *their* heritage? This is a good tack to take, first, because it underlines the point that patristic theology is embedded in history; second, because it demonstrates that the processes of transmission were already in place during the ancient period; and third, because it illustrates the attitudes of the later Fathers to the earlier Fathers, with special reference to errors found in earlier theological writings.

Paying attention to the details of how the Church's heritage is transmitted from Father to Father helps us to understand that theology does not consist in a static body of propositions that attained perfection centuries ago as "timeless insight into God," one capable of reception by future Christians struggle-free. No inert edifice is available for pious (but mindless) transferral, preserved without effort against the ravages of time. Engaging in theology is a strenuous task for us today just as it was for the Fathers long ago. Paying attention also inoculates against a kind of nostalgia for "simpler times." As we shall see, the Fathers faced complex dilemmas about how to assimilate what they received, dilemmas no less perplexing than our own. There is much to learn from their sophisticated processes of discernment—and their deep sense of charity.

We have a great deal of evidence of that process—so much, in fact, that we can only consider a few particular cases. But these cases will be enough to substantiate the claims made in chapter 1 that patristic theology is a dynamic form of activity that has been passed down over the generations. Transmission and appropriation within the patristic heritage have been lively and challenging processes from antiquity.

## The Fathers reading the Fathers

Our examples will be taken from three authors (one Latin, two Greek) who lived across the Mediterranean region over a span of nearly four and a half centuries. Two of these cases are interesting because they demonstrate ways in which well-known fathers could react to earlier well-known fathers. The third additionally reveals how a well-educated theologian in the early middle ages looked back over the early period and worked up a method (admittedly, a rudimentary one) of coping with differences between the fathers—and even with instances when a given father had clearly been in the wrong.

### St Vincent of Lérins

Our first case study centers on St Vincent of Lérins, a Latin theologian who wrote in the first half of the fifth century and is best remembered for the so-called "Canon of St Vincent," which establishes that the standard of orthodox belief is holding to "that which has been believed everywhere, always, by all."[1] This general rule has been often repeated, and much historical research into Vincent and his writings has been built on the supposition that he was trenchantly conservative. So it may come as a surprise that he also offered a less well-known, but quite detailed, account of the nature of progress within orthodox belief, which is "of such sort that it is a true advance, and not a change, in the Faith."[2] Vincent's explanation moves from reiterating that doctrine is essentially changeless, to characterizing the permissible "advances":

---

[1] Vincent of Lérins, *Commonitory* 2.6; trans. T. H. Bindley, *The Commonitory of St Vincent of Lérins*, Early Christian Classics (London: SPCK, 1914), p. 26.

[2] Vincent, *Commonitory* 23.54; trans. Bindley, p. 89.

Truly the Church of Christ, the diligent and cautious Guardian of the doctrines entrusted to her, never changes anything in them, diminishes anything, adds anything; she cuts not off what is necessary, adds not what is superfluous; doth not lose her own, nor take possession of another's; but, *while dealing faithfully and wisely with ancient doctrines, takes pains with and polishes anything in antiquity that lacks shape and finish, consolidates and strengthens anything that is plain and clear, safeguards anything that is established and defined.*[3]

An *advance*, then, as opposed to a *change*, works out an implicit but inchoate teaching, without compromising what is already "plain and clear" and all the while retaining whatever has already been established. By implication, a *change* violates this norm—either by introducing something entirely new, or else by contradicting what is already manifest, or even by abandoning an established definition. According to Vincent not all variations that occur through time are changes (which are by definition illegitimate): some of them are advances (which are by definition legitimate). The examples that Vincent gives to illustrate an advance come from the councils of the church, when occasionally it was necessary to introduce a new word "for the better understanding, never for a new interpretation of the Faith."[4]

On the basis of this distinction, Vincent was prepared to denounce heresy. At several points in his book, he makes strident remarks about Novatian, Photinus, Sabellius, Donatus, Arius, Eunomius,

---

[3]Vincent, *Commonitory* 23.59, emphasis added; trans. Bindley, p. 93.

[4]Ibid.; trans. Bindley, p. 94.

Macedonius, Apollinarius, Priscillian, Jovinian, and Nestorius.[5] He was particularly scathing about Pelagius, Celestius and like-minded Christians: ". . . certain frogs, fleas and short-lived flies, such as are the Pelagians, cry in opposition."[6] He called attention in particular to heretical attempts to garner support for their teachings by interpreting Scripture in ways that he found to be misleading, capricious, and dishonest. On the other hand, Vincent praised stalwart teachers of the church such as Sts Ambrose, Athanasius of Alexandria, Basil the Great, Cyprian of Carthage, Cyril of Alexandria, Felix of Rome, Gregory of Nazianzus, Gregory of Nyssa, Hilary of Poitiers, Julius of Rome, Peter of Alexandria and Theophilus of Alexandria.[7] Their teachings collectively demonstrated the right attitude toward the deposit of the faith: they preserved what has been established, defended the truth and when necessary articulated the unclear.

Vincent's system is very tidy, but he wasn't constrained by it to produce an artificially tidy account of theology. He was willing to address himself to the more complicated case of an eminent, indeed a great, teacher who had erred. And when he did so, he could make some subtle but important distinctions. Let's take three examples: Origen, Tertullian, and Augustine.

A controversy had sprung up around Origen of Alexandria about sixty years before Vincent wrote the *Commonitory*. The main

[5]See Vincent, *Commonitory* 2.5, 4.9–11, 24.62; trans. Bindley, pp. 23–25, 28–31, 96–97.

[6]Vincent, *Commonitory* 9.26 and see also 33.86; trans. Bindley, p. 46 and p. 124.

[7]Vincent, *Commonitory* 5.12, 17.46 and 30.79; trans. Bindley, pp. 31–32, 78–81, 115–17.

agents in the controversy were the redoubtable controversialists and champions of orthodoxy, Sts Jerome and Epiphanius of Salamis. Not for the last time, Origen stood accused of tainting Christianity through his excessive enthusiasm for Hellenistic philosophy. The details of this controversy need not concern us here (not least because, as we shall see, they did not concern Vincent either). But Vincent was clearly aware that Origen had a bad reputation. In fact, Origen is for Vincent the best example of the tragedy of a respected teacher who makes mistakes. Origen's accomplishments garnered him a broad basis of respect. People tend to want to think the best of those whom they admire, since it is easier to think *either* positively *or* negatively about someone. In Vincent's words, "in the Church of God the teacher's error" is "the people's trial," and the trial is "all the greater when the erring one was the more learned."[8]

Vincent enthusiastically admired Origen for his virtuous life—especially his perseverance under Roman judicial torture for being a Christian—and his industry, his numerous and learned writings, his reputation for learning even beyond the Christian community. So impressive are Origen's accomplishments, says Vincent, that one is nearly moved to say, "I prefer to err with Origen than to think rightly with others."[9] (This passage tells us a little something about Vincent's familiarity with Latin philosophy, since it echoes Cicero, probably deliberately, where we read, "By Hercules, I would rather err with Plato than think aright with those others!")[10] But this, says Vincent, would be a grave

[8]Vincent, *Commonitory* 17.42; trans. Bindley, p. 71.

[9]Vincent, *Commonitory* 17.44; trans Bindley, pp. 75–76.

[10]*Tusculan Disputations* I.17.

mistake, and he insists that the "ancient simplicity of the Christian religion" must be preferred even to the prodigious output of a devoted Christian.

Vincent tactfully omits any catalogue of Origen's errors and accepts the possibility that his writings might have been corrupted. In fact, he says he would like to think so himself. This hope is less wishful than it might seem. During Vincent's own time, there were available in Latin competing translations of key works by Origen, like his *On First Principles*. These translations were part of a debate about Origen's orthodoxy. St Jerome accused Rufinus of having prepared a translation that was deliberately misleading, by muting claims that were too speculative for a general audience. With that debate in the air, Vincent's approach is consistent with his scathing reference to those who, like Ham (cf. Gen 9.20–27), not only fail to cover the nakedness of their fathers but even bring attention to it "as something to be laughed at."[11]

Vincent is not as discreet in the chapter following his treatment of Origen, which he dedicates to a Latin theologian who was similarly brilliant but flawed: Tertullian. After alluding to Tertullian's major works in defense of Christianity against numerous religious communities "whose blasphemies he overthrew with the numerous and mighty piles of his volumes as if with so many thunderbolts," Vincent says exactly what was wrong with Tertullian: his alleged defection from the Church to the "New Prophecy" of Montanus.[12] An ascetical movement that sought to reform the Church to pure, primitive discipline, the "New Prophecy" or Montanism has recently been described as "a conservation of

---

[11]Vincent, *Commonitory* 7.19; trans. Bindley, p. 40.

[12]Vincent, *Commonitory* 18.46; trans. Bindley, pp. 79–80.

primitive Christianity in the face of ecclesiastical secularization and imperial persecution."[13]

Vincent is somewhat elliptical here. He does not go into detail about exactly what he found objectionable about Montanus' teachings and practices. Perhaps the problem was that Montanism disrupted the faith. If so, Vincent was objecting to a movement that sought to "revert" to a past that was largely imaginary. There is no need to try to piece together Vincent's attitude toward Tertullian. It is the difference in how Vincent presents Tertullian and how he presents Origen that matters: Vincent admires both, but straightforwardly denounces Tertullian while equivocating about Origen. All of this suggests that Vincent's warm commendation of Origen's life and his work for the Church was authentic.

The third and final example from Vincent to be considered is his attitude toward Augustine of Hippo. With the exception of some interesting lengthy quotations, Vincent says nothing directly about Augustine, so we have to proceed with care—all the more so because there is a traditional bias toward thinking of Vincent as an opponent of the novelties he allegedly found in Augustine's writings.[14] This traditional interpretation is increasingly untenable because of recently rediscovered writings by Vincent, as we will see. First, we need to set out the received opinion about Vincent.

---

[13]R. D. Butler, *The New Prophecy & "New Visions"* (Washington, DC: Catholic University of America Press, 2005), p. 21.

[14]See further A. Casiday, "Vincent of Lérins's *Commonitorium, Objectiones,* and *Excerpta.* Responding to Augustine's Legacy in Fifth-Century Gaul," in A. Hwang et al., eds., *Grace for Grace: The Debates after Augustine and Pelagius* (Washington, DC: Catholic University of America Press, forthcoming).

There is a long-standing practice of interpreting *Commonitory* 26.69, in which Vincent rails against unnamed parties who claim to enjoy "a certain great and special and indeed personal grace of God" that keeps them from moral failure, and even obviates the need for exertion, as a covert attack against Augustine. The idea behind this interpretation is that Vincent was quietly reacting against Augustine's teaching of predestination, signaling his target by mentioning "grace." Vincent was covert because (so the thinking goes) Augustine was too big a target for him to attack directly. Vincent's position on grace, on this reading, is "Semi-Pelagian." That means he is supposed to have attributed the acting of faith neither entirely to human effort, as with the Pelagians, nor entirely to divine grace, as with the Augustinians.

In support of the idea that Vincent was opposed to Augustine's teachings on grace, modern interpreters have frequently referred to Vincent's *Objections*. This document consists of a series of objectionable propositions that imply fatalism and thus undermine freedom, the absurdity of which Vincent draws out clearly. The odd thing about the text is that the *Objections* come down to us embedded in a refutation of them, prepared by Prosper of Aquitaine, who was himself an outspoken advocate of what he himself called "the full doctrine of grace." The habit of reading Vincent as a harsh critic of Augustine, in other words, is circumstantial, propped up by doubtful presumptions, and only advocated by a contemporary who had a vested interest in emphasizing Augustine's teachings at all costs. It would be difficult to fabricate such a pathetic intellectual pedigree.

But what need is there for dismantling bad scholarship? The idea that Vincent was sniping at Augustine is out of step with Vincent's approach to problematical teachers, as we have seen from the *Commonitory*. Even more importantly, the idea that Vincent was an enemy of Augustine is overthrown by the evidence from a recently rediscovered writing by Vincent: his *Excerpts*. This book is apparently a fulfillment of the aspiration that Vincent expressed at the end of his treatment of the unity of Christ, where he writes, "This has been said by way of a digression: at another time, if God will, these points shall be more expansively treated and explained."[15] The *Excerpts* is an expansive treatment and orthodox explanation of Christology. As the name indicates, it is a collection of excerpts. What is surprising in view of the widespread presupposition that Vincent was opposed to Augustine is that all of the excerpts that make it up are taken from Augustine's writings.

Even more tellingly, two of Vincent's excerpts come from Augustine's *On the gift of perseverance* and *On the merits of sins and their remission*. This is noteworthy because Augustine wrote both of those books and dispatched them to Southern Gaul, where Vincent lived, expressly to respond to concerns there about his teachings on grace and freedom. If the old assumptions about Vincent's anti-Augustinianism were correct, then we would expect him to denounce these books, even if only covertly. And yet Vincent takes extracts from them and integrates those extracts into a sophisticated theological account of Christ that is in many key ways more Augustinian than Augustine himself.[16]

For instance, Vincent straightforwardly asserts that "Jesus was assumed in a unique way, predestined in a unique way" (*Excerpts*

[15]Vincent, *Commonitory* 16.41; trans. Bindley, p. 71.

[16]See further A. Casiday, "Grace and the humanity of Christ according to St Vincent of Lérins," *Vigiliae Christianae* 59 (2005): 298–314.

8). Here, Vincent uses the language of "assumption" to describe the way in which, at the Incarnation, the "Lord's human" was *taken up* by God the Word. That sort of language, which was unexceptional in its time, was subsequently abandoned as imprecise and potentially misleading. Talking of "assumption" could give the appearance of suggesting the independent existence of a human person who was taken into a relationship with God. But Latin polemics against Nestorius, especially those written by theologians who themselves used the language of the "assumed man," make it abundantly clear that this is not what was meant. The problem from our point of view is that early Christian Latin lacked the abstract noun *humanitas* ("humanity"), which would clarify that it was humanity and not a human person that was assumed.

Also noteworthy is Vincent's description of Jesus Christ, and more immediately important with reference to Vincent's attitude toward Augustine, is Vincent's use here of the language of "predestination." By using the term "predestined" alongside the term "assumed," Vincent precludes any misunderstanding along the lines we have just considered. If Christ in his humanity was both predestined and assumed, then it is impossible that before the Incarnation there was a human person (Jesus) who had some antecedent merit that God rewarded by bestowing upon that human person the grace of union with God. To put it another way, through using both of those terms Vincent is explaining that before the Incarnation there was no human Christ and thus that the Incarnation cannot possibly be accounted for in terms of antecedent human merit.

From time to time, we read of Vincent that he was full of admiration for Augustine's teachings about God and about Christ but had deep reservations when he came to Augustine's teachings about how God relates to humans.[17] In fact, the passage from the *Excerpts* that we have been considering means that we need to rethink that claim. That passage shows that Vincent was willing to use Augustinian language about how God relates to humans precisely in order to explain the unique instance in which divinity and humanity were related in Christ. Maybe Vincent's silence about the overall trajectory of Augustinian theology is telling, or maybe not. But on the basis of the *Excerpts* we can say with some confidence more about his approach to Augustine's works. Vincent took from Augustine's theological writings the concept of predestination—a concept that, according to the classical readings of the *Commonitory*, Vincent could have considered an illegitimate *change*—and made use of it to propose an *advance* in Christology.

Let's review what we have seen from our study of Vincent's writings. First, he did not intend his famous canon of orthodoxy to preclude advances in faithfully articulating the theological tradition. However appealing Vincent's formula might be to conservatives, Vincent himself clearly believed that better, clearer language can be used in theology. His use of Augustine's writings in the *Excerpts* gives us evidence of how Vincent himself practiced the process of faithfully articulating theology. As for his opposition to change (which, as we have seen, is a technical term and does not refer indiscriminately to all variations through time), we have found that he was able to be appropriately critical in evaluating alleged instances of change.

[17]For example, J. Madoz, *Excerpta Vincentii Lirinis según el códice de Ripoll, n. 151* (Madrid: Editorial Aldecoa, 1940) and also his *El concepto de la Tradición en S. Vicente de Lerins* (Rome: Gregorianum, 1933), pp. 59–89.

We have also seen that Vincent was prepared to be patient, to work carefully through the writings of a flawed but great teacher (Origen). He was also candid enough to acknowledge that the flaws of a great teacher are all the more damaging because of his very greatness. Vincent became combative only after the mind of the Church had been made known, especially through councils but also through customary usage. His major concern is not fault-finding; it is exhorting his readers to prefer God's Church to any one of its members. Importantly, even when doing so, Vincent is not confrontational. His agenda, it seems, is to praise what is good and to pass over any shame of the Fathers as Shem and Japheth had done.

## St Maximus the Confessor

The second of our case studies takes us forward nearly two hundred years to the *Ambigua* by St Maximus the Confessor (580–662). The *Ambigua*, or "Book of Difficulties" or "Perplexities," is a compilation of Maximus' responses (c. 628–30) to queries that were put to him by Archbishop John of Cyzicus, and later (around 634) by an otherwise unknown Thomas. In these responses, Maximus re-deployed a massive complex of theological writings from the past in a way that would be comprehensible in terms of current debates. Most of the *Ambigua* are concerned in one way or another with the theological legacy that came down from Origen of Alexandria.

Modern experts, such as Hans Urs von Balthasar, Polycarp Sherwood, Paul Blowers, and Andrew Louth, regard *Ambiguum* 7 ("On the Beginnings and End of Rational Creatures") in particular as a watershed in the theological refutation of Origenist errors.

Maximus' reading for this *Ambiguum* is a passage from Gregory's *Oration* 14.7, in which Gregory poses the question, "Is it God's intention that we who are a portion of God and have slipped down from above should out of self-importance be so haughty and puffed up as to despise our Creator?"[18]

Gregory's own answer is a resounding "Not at all!" But what Gregory is rejecting is precisely our haughtiness and what goes with it. His breezy comment about our being "a portion of God" and having "slipped down from above out of self-importance" is left unqualified. And that lack of qualification is what troubles Maximus. He immediately distances himself from those who seek from the words of Gregory support for their belief that originally "there once existed a single unity (ἑνάς) of rational beings," that we are connatural with God, and that bodies were formed by God in order to punish the transgression whereby rational beings defected from that original unity.[19] This strange set of ideas about the "first things" calls for comment.

Well over a generation before Maximus' birth, Cyril of Scythopolis reported that controversies began in Palestine in the monastery founded by St Sabas. When Cyril reports his meeting with the venerable old monk Cyriacus, he says that these words from Gregory of Nazianzus' *Ad Eunomium* 12 (also *Oration* 27) are invoked by those who are speculating about theological matters: "Philosophize about the world, matter, the soul, the good and the evil rational natures, the Resurrection and the Passion of Christ; for

---

[18]St. Maximus the Confessor, *On the Cosmic Mystery of Jesus Christ*, trans. Paul Blowers and Robert Wilken (Crestwood, NY: St Vladimir's Seminary Press, 2003), p. 45.

[19]Maximus, *Ambiguum* 7.1; trans. Blowers and Wilken, p. 45.

in these matters hitting on the truth is not without profit and error is without danger."[20] Cyriacus lacked the intellectual finesse and the deference to Gregory's reputation that Maximus would later demonstrate at some length in *Ambiguum* 7. Instead, he sharply corrects Cyril and, in the process, apparently contradicts Gregory: "The doctrines of pre-existence and restoration are not indifferent and without danger, but dangerous, harmful and blasphemous."[21]

The fact that unwelcome speculation about the origins and the end of creation was flourishing and was seeking to borrow legitimacy from Gregory of Nazianzus is supported also in the correspondence of the "Grand Old Man" of Gaza, Barsanuphius, and the "Other Old Man," John. In *Letter* 604, we read an extremely long discussion of the appropriation of Cappadocian theology (especially the writings by Gregory of Nazianzus and Gregory of Nyssa) to similar ends. This letter is part of a series in which Barsanuphius and John address the problem of what use—if any!—can rightly be made of the writings of Origen and the other noted theologians, Didymus the Blind and Evagrius the Solitary. Barsanuphius responded firmly in the negative, whereas John was guardedly prepared to allow that some good might be found in their pages, though he quickly added that monks had better ways to spend their time.

Not all discussions on this topic were so civilized. Returning to Cyril's account, we read of the outbreak of physical violence. A monk called Nonnus began to propagate theological speculation

---

[20]Cyril of Scythopolis, *Life of Cyriacus* 12, in *The Lives of the Monks of Palestine*, Cistercian Studies 114, trans. R. Price (Kalamazoo, MI: Cistercian Publications, 1991), p. 253.

[21]Ibid.

along these lines in the New Lavra shortly after the death of St Sabas. The teaching spread throughout the monastic population of Palestine. The strife between the monks was so great that eventually fighting broke out around the Great Lavra. For a time, the Great Lavra itself was taken over by Nonnus and likeminded monks. But their hold over the Lavra was short-lived as they began to argue amongst themselves about esoteric points of doctrine (as heretics will do). These events, according to Cyril, prompted the condemnation of Origen at the Fifth Ecumenical Council.[22] The emperor, Justinian, was eventually obliged to intervene. Justinian's involvement was decisive and was based on an informed interest in the theological matters being debated. In fact, Justinian's *Letter to Menas* (a major source for his thinking on the subject) preserves a passage, apparently from Origen's *On First Principles* 2.2.1, that closely parallels *Ambiguum* 7.1. But despite Justinian's intervention and the total of three theological condemnations, the difficulties were still alive several decades later when Maximus addressed himself to them.

The character of Maximus' response to Gregory's readers is strikingly different to, say, Cyril of Scythopolis' accounts of controversies in the Palestinian monasteries. Cyril uses the word "Origenist" promiscuously but has very little to say about the doctrines that were so abhorrent to him. He does include a catalogue of esoteric beliefs at *Life of Cyriacus* 12–13, but it is unclear that this passage describes an actual system of doctrine, let alone represents accurately what the "Origenists" believed. (It may be a caricature.) There is abundant anecdotal evidence that these "Origenists" were drawing inspiration from Gregory. With that in mind, the

---

[22]Cyril of Scythopolis, *Life of Sabas* 83–90, in *The Lives of the Monks of Palestine,* trans. Price, pp. 196–209.

impression given by Cyril's *Lives* is that Cyril was keen to shield Gregory from any hint of impropriety by identifying Origen, an earlier theologian who was already known to be controversial, as the cause of all the problems.

For his part, Maximus' explanation of Gregory is subtler and more patient. He brings to his solution other passages from Gregory— and from Dionysius the Areopagite, too—and makes a reasoned case for his position. He does not rely on an emotive response to Origen's reputation to see him through, in the way that Cyriacus had done. Instead, he thinks carefully through Gregory's writings and offers a reading of them that is consonant with contemporary theological concerns and respectable with reference to contemporary theological standards.

In the scholarly conversations, Maximus' work is often held up as a prime example of the domestication of Origen's theology. There is undoubted merit in reading his *Ambigua* in that way. But before we move to another instance of the reception of patristic works by Fathers, we should spare a moment to reflect on one aspect of the scholarly discussions. Polycarp Sherwood's pioneering study of the *Ambigua* indicates by its very title what he thought Maximus was doing: *The Earlier Ambigua of Saint Maximus the Confessor and His Refutation of Origenism*. With some trepidation, I would suggest that Maximus was not refuting Origenism. True, there are entrenched habits of thinking that Origenism means that particular combination of metaphysical claims that were condemned by Emperor Justinian and company. But why abandon Origen's works to be abused by philosophically unsound and theologically corrupt monks? No, Maximus wasn't refuting Origenism. He wasn't even really retrieving Origen (as though

Origen had somehow been kidnapped by heretics and needed rescuing). Rather, I suggest that Maximus was preserving the valuable insights from Origen that Gregory had already embraced and he was legitimating them for further consideration.

## The "Filioque"

For our final case study, we will again move forward two centuries to consider events that occurred in the midst of another controversy—but this time there is a striking difference in the controversy itself. Our first example (from St Vincent of Lérins) was a Latin theological response to ideas that came from a range of sources, Latin as well as Greek. Vincent's response demonstrated a real, if perhaps underdeveloped, sense for critically responding to erroneous teachings that were problematic because they had been advanced by respected teachers.

Our second example (from St Maximus the Confessor) was chosen from the early stages of Maximus' theological writings, when he was disambiguating a passage from Gregory of Nazianzus' writings. Already at this point, Maximus' preoccupation with Christology was becoming apparent, but in his later writings Maximus explicitly addressed himself to the debate about whether in Christ there are two wills or whether there is only one will. Now Maximus was exiled to the West and he spent time in North Africa and also in Rome. Although our case study was taken from a debate about matters internal to Greek theology, Maximus' latter writings were part of a multilateral resistance to imperially sponsored theology. He joined with Pope Martin to argue against the teaching that there was in Christ only one will. Both Maximus and Martin were abused, even tortured, by political authorities for their resistance to imperial doctrine and both died as a result of those abuses. So in this case the illustrious Greek Father fought alongside the Pope of Rome against the Emperor.

But in our third and final example, the debate itself pits the Church of Constantinople against the Church of Rome. It is no overstatement to say that this debate is a major turning point in the estrangement between the Christian West and the Christian East. It is a debate over the Latin insertion into the confession of a word into the clauses about the Holy Spirit—*Filioque* ("and [from] the Son")—that indicates that the Spirit proceeds from the Son as well as the Father. This debate has many components, which have been argued at different times. For example, it has been objected that the Church of Rome has no right to modify unilaterally a creed that was formulated by an ecumenical council. Or again it has been argued that the doctrine itself is simply wrong with respect to the Trinity. What is of interest to us in this debate, though, is another matter. This time, we are going to see how a learned theologian reacts to cases where the Fathers seem to disagree amongst themselves.

It is a fact of history that the theological literature of antiquity provides evidence which can be taken to support either the dual procession of the Holy Spirit (called "filioquism") or the procession of the Holy Spirit from the Father alone (called "patrimonism"). The origins of this difference are obscure. One thing is clear: the creedal affirmation of the Spirit's dual procession was centuries old by the time it caused controversies. The earliest occurrence known to me dates to 410, when the Nicene Creed was recited at the Synod of Seleucia-Ctesiphon. The Syriac version includes an unexpected reference to "the living Paraclete who is from the Father and the Son" (ÍÎFP BFÍ rd Bd ÍÔd ÉÎÅ).[23] Perhaps this translation is an indirect witness to a base text in Greek that affirmed the dual procession of the Holy Spirit. And if so, perhaps that text also circulated in the West, where it may have contributed to the inclusion of the significant clause into the Latin version. This is, however, conjecture. In any case, the survival of the Syriac version pushes back the earliest known occurrence by over 150 years. Excluding the evidence from the Council of Ctesiphon-Seleucia, the next earliest appearance known to us comes from late fifth-century Spain.

There, Catholic Christian bishops were confronted by conquering Germanic tribes who had been converted to Christianity by Ulfilas, "the Apostle of the Goths." Abundant contemporary and near-contemporary records about Ulfilas—a letter by Auxentius, and the *Church Histories* by Philostorgius, Socrates, Sozomen, and Theodoret—agree that Ulfilas' Christology was in line with Arius' Christology. Given this connection, the Spanish bishops would have naturally considered the Visigothic settlers and overlords of the Iberian Peninsula to be Arian heretics. It is widely assumed that the Spanish bishops added to the creed the clause about the Son's role in the procession of the Holy Spirit, so that it would be inescapably clear that the Son is fully divine in precisely the same way that the Father is fully divine.

---

[23]The text and translation are from A. Vööbus, "New Sources for the Symbol in Early Syrian Christianity," *Vigiliae Christianae* 26 (1974): 291–96. On this council and its translation of the creed, see also J. Gribomont, "Le Symbole de foi de Séleucie-Ctésiphon (410)," in R. Fischer, ed., *A Tribute to Arthur Vööbus* (Chicago: Lutheran School of Theology, 1977), pp. 283–94; and A. de Halleux, "Le symbole des évêques perses au synode de Séleucie-Ctésiphon (410)," in G. Wiessner, ed., *Erkenntnisse und Meinungen* (Wiesbaden: Harrassowitz, 1973–1978), vol. 2, pp. 161–90.

Theological arguments in support of this view are available from a variety of patristic sources—not just Latin, but Greek sources, too (and keeping in mind the translation of the Creed from Persia, perhaps Syriac sources as well). By Photius' time, collections of excerpts from authoritative texts were in circulation. These collections made it easier for both sides to argue that their understanding was supported by the Fathers. The ninth century debates over the *Filioque* therefore give us an opportunity to study the position taken by the patriarch of Constantinople, St Photius the Great, on the problem of conflicting patristic authorities.

Photius was a highly educated layman with good connections in the upper echelons of the Imperial Court who was made patriarch in the midst of controversy. The sitting patriarch, Ignatius, had run afoul of powerful figures and was deposed, so Photius was rapidly ordained through ecclesiastical ranks and installed as patriarch in 858. Ignatius' supporters objected to anyone who would listen. They received a sympathetic hearing from Pope Nicholas I. At first, Nicholas declined to be involved in the debates. But as a stalwart advocate of papal primacy, the Pope soon had his own reasons for conflict with Photius: both Rome and Constantinople were laying claim to jurisdictional oversight of the recently converted Bulgaria. Open conflict was always a possibility. When the conflict broke, a number of identifiable areas for debate were provided by the fact that the missionaries from the East and from the West (particularly from what is now German-speaking Europe) were bringing different observances to the Balkans. These differences ranged from the fairly superficial (about manner of clerical dress), through the social (about the rules for fasting), to the theological (about the doctrine of the Trinity).

Not surprisingly, this latter was the most provocative divergence. The Carolingians included in the Nicene Creed the clause "and the Son." By the time the Carolingians were teaching the expanded creed to the Bulgarians, it was widely accepted as a traditional article of the faith in the Latin Christian world. This is not to say that everyone in the West supported the inclusion of the *Filioque* in the creed. Enthusiasm for modifying the creed came from the North, but several popes met this enthusiasm with a perceptible coolness. It was not for Frankish upstarts to explain good liturgical practice to the Holy See. Even so, records from the period—such a conference that Pope Leo III held with a deputation from Aachen, as reported by Smaragdus—show us that some western theologians were supportive of the theological claims implied by the *Filioque,* but nevertheless explicitly rejected any modification to the creed. It took several centuries of tacit acceptance of the doctrine of the dual procession before that clause was formally inserted into the creed and recited liturgically in Rome itself.

What seems to have held back this development was a common understanding of the seventh canon of the Third Ecumenical Council (Ephesus, 431). That canon says that no one is "to bring forward, or to write, or to compose a different Faith (πίστιν ἐτέραν) as a rival to that established by the holy Fathers assembled with the Holy Spirit in Nicaea"[24] and it stipulates disciplinary measures to be taken if anyone does so. There is an extremely old tradition of seeing in this canon a prohibition of any change to the text of the Nicene-Constantinopolitan Creed. This deference has been detected in Leo III's position and it is unquestionably an important part of the Greek response to the alteration of the

---

[24]Canon seven of the Third Ecumenical Council; trans. NPNF, second series, vol. 14, p. 231 (translation slightly modified).

Creed. In Orthodox Christendom, tremendous significance was already being ascribed to the acts of the Ecumenical Councils, even in cases where those councils were without great impact when they occurred.

Meanwhile, the Carolingians were busy tracing a genealogy of Trinitarian theology that supported their position, by generating lists of patristic sources to support the dual procession of the Holy Spirit. They relied chiefly on the Latin Fathers, though they were not unaware of the theology of the Greek Fathers. A good example is Theodulf of Orléans's *On the Holy Spirit,* in which he appeals to Athanasius the Great, Didymus the Blind, Gregory of Nazianzus, Cyril of Alexandria, and Hilary of Poitiers, amongst others. The Carolingian project did not go unchallenged. Photius' *Mystagogy of the Holy Spirit* is a direct rebuttal. Photius reports that his adversaries defended their position by invoking Ambrose, Augustine, and Jerome, claiming,

> One ought not to charge the sacred Fathers with the crime of ungodliness. Either one agrees with their opinion because they taught piously and are acknowledged as Fathers, or they, together with their teaching, should be rejected as impious because they introduced godless doctrines.[25]

Photius makes a counter-argument to this claim, indicating on two fronts that it is untenably crude. First, it presumes that teaching is either absolutely pure or else absolutely impure and so compels assent or rejection, respectively. Second, it asserts that those acknowledged as holy Fathers are therefore to be followed in every particular.

[25]Photius, *On the Mystagogy of the Holy Spirit* 66, trans. Holy Transfiguration Monastery (Studion Publishers, 1983).

Photius responds by criticizing the Carolingians for opposing patristic excerpts to "the teaching of the Church." In contrast to the unduly simplistic assertion that the teaching of a saint must be absolutely pure, Photius clearly accepts that error (even "godless error") is, from time to time, found in the teachings of those who, he says, "were admirable by reason of many other qualities which manifest virtue and piety." So despite their errors, Photius is still willing to acknowledge that they are Fathers.

This wasn't a limp conciliatory gesture. Photius regarded the *Filioque* as a grave error. As he wrote in his *Letter* 13.33: "But also that blasphemy about the Spirit (or rather the Holy Trinity as a whole), which none surpasses, would suffice by itself—even if there were none of the aforementioned effronteries—to earn them a thousand anathemas." His willingness to see people who are mistaken in that way as being nevertheless *fathers* is particularly disarming. But it isn't just a tactical maneuver to give him an advantage in the argument. As his treatise goes on, he makes it apparent that there is an overarching principle that explains how he can simultaneously abominate blasphemy and still honor fathers who err. He accepts that a venerable father is not *ipso facto* inerrant, that a saint can be in error, and that holiness is distinguishable from accuracy. He even explicitly acknowledges that Greek Fathers are known to have erred (*Mystagogy* 75; *Letter* 24.21) and this, too, is disarmingly candid—not to mention unexpected, since Photius was a great advocate of the putative superiority of Greek in contrast to the "impoverished" Latin language (*Mystagogy* 55; *Letter* 24.5)!

The key is Photius' belief that we have the great benefit of hindsight with respect to theology through history (calling it historical development might not be too much), and his recognition that as Christians we are obliged to be charitable. First, as we have seen, he accepts in matters of doctrine that standards of precision increase over time. In his terms, an awareness of precise standards—even when it comes in the form of having one's mistakes corrected!—is the "benefit of advantage" that moderns have in comparison to ancients (see *Mystagogy* 68). In hindsight, we can identify ambiguities that may have been perfectly innocent in their time but that nevertheless went on to inspire heretical developments.

That basically psychological point is not the limit to Photius' claim. He was well versed in classical and patristic literature and from study of that literature he obviously came to understand that there are legitimate developments in the course of history. This awareness made him able to acknowledge that changing circumstances may invalidate earlier views, but it also enabled him to respond in an insightful way (rather than with uncritical hostility) toward those who held the invalidated views. This is a major step in Photius' polemic against the *Filioque* toward a critical approach to the reception of earlier theology that accepts the importance of development over time.

As for charity in interpretation, it is precisely for failure in this area that he faults the Frankish theologians: "But if they [i.e., the Latin Fathers] in no manner shared the benefit of your advantages, why do you introduce their human defect as a mandate for your blasphemous belief?" (*Mystagogy* 68). Of those earlier fathers, Photius says that they were unlike the Frankish theologians, since they did not violate Our Lord's promise to his disciples: "But when the Comforter is come, whom I will send unto you from the Father, even the Spirit of truth, which proceeds from the Father, he shall testify of me" (Jn 15.26; cf. *Mystagogy* 69). Because the Fathers' teachings can be reconciled to the Lord's teaching without doing any violence to either, those Fathers have no share in the anathema that befalls Photius' contemporaries. Photius' argument here is dense and it needs to be unpacked.

In this context, the allusion to John's Gospel indicates that Photius is identifying two movements of the Spirit that are distinguishable by their causation: the sending of the Spirit by the Son, and the proceeding of the Spirit from the Father. If we keep these two movements in mind, we can appreciate Photius' distinction between the Fathers and the Carolingians. Photius suggests that the patristic doctrine refers to the Son sending the Spirit from the Father in the economy of salvation, which is how he interprets John 15.26. If we take that "economic" interpretation as the key to understanding references to dual procession when we encounter them in writings by the Fathers, we can reconcile those passages to the teaching that the eternal procession of the Spirit is from the Father alone. By contrast, the Carolingians' teaching does not admit of being construed in that way. Indeed, in Photius' account the Carolingians come in for criticism precisely because they conflate these two distinct movements of the Spirit and take John 15.26 as evidence for the eternal, dual procession of the Holy Spirit.

It would take us too far from our topic to verify Photius' case by comparing it to the patristic evidence that was being debated in his day. Maybe his construal of the excerpts from Latin theology has merit. Perhaps attentive reading of the key passages would vindicate Photius' claim that they speak in one way about the eternal procession of the Holy Spirit, and another way about the economic procession of the Holy Spirit. For my part, I doubt whether such an interpretation would hold up for all of the evidence. Photius' theory seems to attribute to the Latin Fathers a level of success in avoiding unseen pitfalls that is preternatural and that strains credibility. As an attempt to identify consensus over centuries, it is ingenious. The very success of that approach, however, raises at least the possibility that what has actually happened is Photius has generated an appearance of consensus.

Be that as it may, what primarily interests us here is not so much the factual accuracy of Photius' claims about Latin patristics, as it is the way that Photius takes historical development seriously as part of his approach to seeming conflict amongst the fathers. His indications, too, that saintliness does not entail inerrancy are also important. The idea that saints are always right, and therefore always necessarily agree amongst themselves, about the most important matters is something Photius abandoned. He distinguished holiness from uniformity. And he did so largely as a way to challenge an unwholesome approach to the Christian heritage, one that attempts to homogenize it entirely so that it corresponds exactly to and vindicates some specific contemporary position. (Photius himself was not immune to the appeal of reading a modern distinction back into an ancient writing, if I am right in my suppositions about his neat usage of John 15.26 to resolve difficulties.)

Photius takes his challenge to Carolingian historical theology even further. Photius accepts that any particular Father could perhaps have erred in this important matter, but falls back on the sanctity of a holy life (rather than on relentless doctrinal precision) to explain why we regard that person as a Father. In doing so, he makes behavior a factor in his debate with the Carolingians.

He can draw a contrast between an innocent mistake made by a holy person, and a polemical argument made by an irresponsible person. According to Photius, drawing attention to an ancient error is itself culpable—and so trying to build on that error, thus compounding the error, is all the more culpable. With reference to the trope from Genesis 9 familiar to us from Vincent's *Commonitory*, Photius bluntly says that the Carolingians are more accursed than Ham, because the Carolingians actually went further than Ham by *uncovering* their fathers and only then announcing their nakedness to the whole world (*Mystagogy* 70).

## Reading the Fathers with the Fathers

This chapter began by asking how the heritage is transmitted. Instead of giving an abstract answer to that question, we have looked first at several historical examples that illustrate the process at work. These case studies have brought to our attention that transformations occur as patristic theological writings are appropriated generations, or even centuries, after they were written. By looking at the appropriation of patristic theology, we have shifted our attention: in the first chapter, we were primarily interested in the sources of patristic theology, and in this chapter, we have been primarily interested in its recipients. Of course, the recipients that we have studied here are unusual in that they are themselves now recognized as Fathers of the Church. This doesn't mean that their practices are somehow impossible for us to imitate—quite the opposite! It actually encourages us to learn how to read the earlier fathers as they did. The ancient legacy of theology is perpetuated down the generations without interruption and we must not be timid about taking our place in that process.

Looking back to the examples that were provided by Sts Vincent of Lérins, Maximus the Confessor, and Photius the Great, we will now venture some general conclusions.

* * *

What do we learn, then, about the transmission of the patristic heritage from Vincent and his writings? The main point that Vincent repeatedly makes throughout his writings is that our response to theological writings must be based solidly on fundamental principles. He elaborates these principles at length in the *Commonitory*, where he advances several criteria for determining whether a given theological writing is orthodox. Orthodoxy in a contemporary theologian is recognized, in part, by the compatibility and coherence of that theologian's writings with earlier theological works that have been accepted as orthodox. As he describes it, the process is one in which the Church Herself "while dealing faithfully and wisely with ancient doctrines, takes pains with and polishes anything in antiquity that lacks shape and finish, consolidates and strengthens anything that is plain and clear, safeguards anything that is established and defined."[26]

In a certain sense, orthodox theology is therefore a cumulative undertaking that occurs within the Church. Vincent does not offer a theological analysis of the Church: he takes the Church for granted, and it provides the context within which he reasons. But this gap in Vincent's thinking is problematic. It would be an easy thing to find groups who differ over doctrinal matters, but who could nevertheless honestly subscribe to Vincent's theological project. For instance, in responding to the Bonn Conference in 1874 and 1875, where there were lively debates over the *Filioque,*

[26]Vincent, *Commonitory* 23.59; trans. Bindley, p. 93.

the Anglican participants insisted that the *Filioque* was an important part of the catholic heritage and for that reason should not be abandoned lightly. What happens when different communities tenaciously insist that their beliefs are exactly "that which has been believed everywhere, always, by all"? History does not interpret itself for us. Merely invoking that definition and insisting that it describes one's own beliefs is not an argument. And nor was it an argument when Vincent first framed it.

Vincent's purpose was not to relieve his readers of the burden of making sense of history. He provides criteria for identifying orthodoxy and he also demonstrates how to apply these criteria; in this way, he offers up a theory of theology. His theory incorporates sustained discussion of the perennial question about the "development of doctrine": does doctrine change over time, or is it only formulated in different terms without a change in substance?

The key terms that Vincent uses in that discussion are "advance" and "change." These terms are opposite, the former referring to a legitimate and authentic development with respect to earlier ideas and the latter referring to an illegitimate and inauthentic development. Both of them, then, are types of development. Vincent makes this distinction because he wishes to hold together, on the one hand, his recognition that differences inevitably come in the course of history and, on the other hand, the possibility of meaningfully distinguishing the differences that are good from those that are bad. In other words, Vincent did not naïvely think that orthodox Christian belief exists outside of time and therefore that any difference that occurs is by definition a bad thing. Orthodox theology is dynamic, not static. In historical perspective, this dynamism is more accurately characterized as accumulation than as, say, recapitulation. Along the way, it is possible for a particular theological position to be surpassed without disgrace.

I noted that Vincent's theory presupposes the church instead of including it for detailed consideration. There is a limitation to his thinking that can be seen to relate to that gap. In commenting on Origen, Vincent made too many allowances to the uninformed if he genuinely believed—as he suggests at *Commonitory* 17.45—that Origen's writings had been tampered with. Vincent's theory gives great importance to reputations, without giving adequate attention to the very real possibility that a reputation can be produced from sheerest ignorance. What is to keep dislike from calcifying into prejudice? Once prejudices are entrenched, how can they be dislodged? Vincent's theory of theology raises for explicit consideration the extent to which time-honored claims can become accepted as facts. Where it falls short is its failure to identify which intellectual resources can be used to check, to qualify, or to revise those feelings. He is very good about accounting for how theology is built up as a collective undertaking by the Church, but less impressive when it comes to confronting widespread misunderstandings within the Church.

* * *

Vincent's defense of Origen was rather thin, if not supine; by contrast, Maximus' strategic re-reading of Gregory of Nazianzus seems to have been predicated on the belief that the best defense is a good offense. Within a controversy over the theological legacy of Origen, Maximus was responding to the way that passages from Gregory's writings were being used to support a speculative, allegorical program of reading scripture common to the great Alexandrian exegetes of Scripture (especially Origen, Didymus, and

Evagrius, though hearkening back also to Philo). His critique of this program was not an appeal to the authority of tradition. His responses in the *Ambigua* are not a matter of simplistically asserting that Gregory was always correct and that the standard of correctness is that standard which Maximus identifies as Orthodoxy. Instead, Maximus argues at some length that Gregory's would-be interpreters are philosophically inept and do not understand basic philosophical terms, such as movement, beginning, becoming, and reasons (*logoi*). Their ineptitude leads them into gross errors and so keeps them from understanding the truth.

What Maximus opposed was a metaphysical system that ignored its own philosophical and theological consequences, with the results that the basic principles of Christian theology were compromised. The clearest example of this concern is found in the condemnation of the proposition that, at the resurrection, the bodies that arise will be spherical in shape. I am not aware of evidence that anyone actually posited that claim; what it seems to express is anxiety about the overwhelming of a Christian doctrine (namely, that the resurrected body will be perfect) by a Pythagorean doctrine (namely, that the sphere is the perfect shape).

Another example is provided in Maximus' *Ambiguum* 7, where he attributes to his anonymous opponents the belief that "as rational beings were dispersed in various ways, God envisaged the creation of this corporeal world to unite them with bodies as punishment for their former transgressions."[27] The implication that God created bodies as part of a divine regime of punishment offends against the sense that God's creation is "very good" (Gen 1.31). But it is not at all clear that it was Origen's own perspective,

---

[27]Maximus, *Ambiguum* 7.1; trans. Blowers and Wilken, pp. 45–46.

according to which bodies are a safety net rather than a punishment. Just because a safety net isn't a hammock does not make it a punishment. As Origen explains, "God had foreknowledge of the differences that were to arise among souls or spiritual powers, in order to arrange that each in proportion to its merits might wear a different bodily covering of this or that quality."[28] Origen is no doubt bold to hypothesize about bodies of different qualities being apportioned to pre-incarnated souls "in proportion to their merits," but this simply does not imply that the bodies are punitive.

To fill in the gap of evidence, some scholars of Maximus' writings have attributed these views to Evagrius Ponticus and on that basis identified Evagrius' writings as the target for Maximus' theological adjustments. For example, Maximus says of an unmistakably Aristotelian definition that it "is correct even though it was spoken by an outsider."[29] Polycarp Sherwood has alleged that the definition has been taken from an unidentified writing by Evagrius and then made a fuss over the implication that Maximus would have referred to Evagrius as an "outsider."[30] This is a bad reading based on the purely conjectural supposition that Maximus for whatever reason was quoting Evagrius' writings deliberately in order to reject them.

There is nothing in Maximus' writings that actually says anything remotely like, "Now we need to decontaminate Origen's

[28]Origen, *On First Principles* 4.4.8, trans. G. W. Butterworth (Gloucester, MA: Peter Smith, 1973), p. 325.

[29]Maximus, *Ambiguum* 7.1; trans. Blowers and Wilken, p. 48.

[30]Polycarp Sherwood, *The Earlier Ambigua of Saint Maximus the Confessor and His Refutation of Origenism* (Rome: Herder, 1955), p. 100.

and Evagrius' writings since they are so philosophical, and to integrate some emotional and Biblical spirituality into Orthodoxy." Reading Maximus' works in that way is a by-product of the twin assumptions that Origen's legacy required purification (i.e., that they were wrong and were recognized as such from the start) and that the Orthodox Fathers set themselves the task of purifying it. Those assumptions are unjustified. Origen's writings and Evagrius' were not the property of heretics, which for some reason the Orthodox decided to retrieve for the good of the Church. Those writings were already part of the literary legacy of the Christian East, much as Gregory's writings were part of that legacy, too.

Maximus' *Ambigua* indicate that what he was interested in doing was keeping Gregory of Nazianzus' works from being used cavalierly by those who "borrowed too much from Greek [i.e., pagan] teachings" to support an esoteric metaphysical system of belief.[31] There is something audacious in what Maximus was up to in laying his claim on Gregory's theology. First, Maximus made a painstaking philosophical argument in which he reduced his adversaries' interpretation of Gregory to absurdity. Maximus does this by building up a fund of Gregory's thoughts which he then uses to exegete the passage under consideration. This move showcases two key features of Maximus' reading of Gregory's works: he reads closely through the corpus (he is not a dilettante, and his reading is not desultory) and he is keenly analytic in his own thinking. He carries his argument forward by compiling parallels from Gregory's other writings that tell against by his adversaries' allegations.

---

[31]Maximus, *Ambiguum* 7.1; trans. Blowers and Wilken, p. 45.

It is relatively easy to explode someone else's work. What is harder is to offer something better. Maximus' next task is to offer an orthodox reading of the disputed passage. His reading is subtle and thorough, resisting satisfactorily summarization, so we will not pursue it in great detail. It suffices to say here that the foundation of Maximus' theological interpretation of Gregory's statement that we "are a portion of God and have slipped down from above" is his own statement that "the one Logos is many *logoi*."[32]

Maximus goes much further in describing the reciprocal relationship that exists between the Logos and the *logoi*—the meanings, or reasons, of created beings. In doing so, Maximus draws freely from ideas developed by earlier theologians. In *Ambiguum* 7 alone, he cites by name Basil the Great, Clement of Alexandria (and, through him, Pantaenus), and Dionysius the Areopagite. Their ideas extend the platform on which Maximus based his interpretation of Gregory and by making use of them in this way Maximus is in effect working up a *consensus patrum* on this topic. In other words, Maximus' interpretation of Gregory proceeds, first, by using Gregory's lucid passages to illuminate Gregory's murky passages and, then, by building up a frame of reference for Gregory's theology out of the writings of other theologians whose authority is acknowledged.

The whole of Maximus' interest in Gregory's theology is not exhausted by these interpretive maneuvers. He is working toward the development of an authentic, contemporary theological voice that resonates with ancient significance. The initial impression given by *Ambiguum* 7 is that Maximus is chiefly concerned to

---

[32]Maximus, *Ambiguum* 7.1; trans. Blowers and Wilken, pp. 54–55.

defend Gregory's reputation. That concern is surely part of what we see in this writing, but in fact something even more sophisticated is going on here. This is less an exercise in text criticism than it is a theological exposition. Attention to the text is fundamental to any respectable exposition, and Maximus' philosophical and comparative studies are satisfactory evidence that he has taken due care to attend diligently to Gregory's *Oration* 14. He goes further, though, in order to engage with the meaning of that oration. He is not treating it as an object of historical interest, but rather is putting himself into an immediate relationship with it.

Maximus' engagement with Gregory's writing demonstrates what T.S. Eliot called "a perception, not only of the pastness of the past, but also of its presence."[33] In reading Gregory's *Oration*, Maximus was open to claims that Gregory's theology made on him as an immediate, present factor. Because he was steeped in Gregory's work, Maximus expresses himself in a theological idiom that shows Gregory's influence. He is so open to tradition that he fairly tends to disappear into it. His language and his style derive considerably from the close, open reading of the *Orations*. True, his interpretation of Gregory's text is embedded in a controversy. But the polemic is merely his initial motive in interpretation. Fairly early on in the *Ambiguum*, he satisfies himself (and attempts to satisfy the reader) that his opponents' reading has been adequately redressed and their errors fairly exposed. But then he goes on to deeper considerations, and here he is moved less by a need to disprove someone else than by a need to understand Gregory. In this way, his own theology comes to be informed by reading Gregory's works (and Dionysius', too).

---

[33]T.S. Eliot, "Tradition and the individual talent," in *The Waste Land and Other Writings* (New York: The Modern Library), pp. 99–108 at p. 100.

In terms of engagement with earlier theological works, Maximus' *Ambigua* is profounder than Vincent's *Excerpts*. In both cases, the author tends to disappear into the flow of earlier language, though the *Ambigua* show the imprint of Maximus' hands to a much greater extent than the *Excerpts* does of Vincent's. This comparison is not to Vincent's detriment: the *Excerpts* is more than an impressively and cleanly assembled cento; it is much more than a clever literary exercise. It is an intelligent theological text in its own right. And nor does Maximus' greater profundity reflect badly on Vincent, since we can if we wish see Maximus' theological exegesis of Gregory as a prime specimen of Vincent's theory of theology at work. Indeed, Vincent's attitude toward the Fathers and how their theology is to be treated provides us a valuable insight into how and why Maximus did what he did in interpreting Gregory.

* * *

In contrast to Vincent's application of Augustinian ideas toward a Christological treatise and to Maximus' interpretation of Gregory that is thoroughly imbued with Gregory's theological sense, what is conspicuous in Photius' polemic about the *Filioque* is that he balances a thorough-going theological rejection of that doctrine and a genuine respect for the fathers whose writings were taken to support that doctrine. We may think back to Vincent's attitude toward Origen. He was enthusiastic about Origen's virtues and impressed by his diligence, but deferential to his critics. Photius is similarly prepared to acknowledge the accomplishments of patristic teachers, but he is also prepared to accept that—indeed, to explain in detail how—some of them were in error.

This is strikingly different to Vincent's coy allusion to problems with Origen. Photius probes the flawed doctrines but insists that such probative treatment is not incompatible with the level of respect that is due to ancient teachers and fathers. His strategy could be called "filial criticism" because he criticizes problematic teachings from earlier theologians while nevertheless accepting that those theologians are to be treated as revered fathers in the faith despite their flaws. He is not abusive in his treatment, nor is he dismissive. He does not suggest that the fact that they made mistakes (even serious mistakes) means that we ought to treat them with contempt.

Photius reserves his harsh words for the Carolingian theologians who were building up a dossier of patristic sources in support of their doctrine that the Holy Spirit proceeds from both the Father and the Son. One of Photius' comments is particularly revealing. He castigates his opponents for failure to learn from mistakes of the past, referring to "the benefit of your advantages." He passes very quickly over this comment, but the general point he is making in that section of the *Mystagogy* is that mistakes have been and still are corrected and that these corrections tend to the improvement of theological conversation.

This point amounts to nothing less than a substantial contribution to the development of a critical sense for theology as an undertaking that has a history. In contesting the Frankish history of dogma, Photius' maneuver is to allow that mistakes have been made and to indicate that the correction of those mistakes is a major element driving forward the "advance" (to revert to Vincent's terminology) of theology. Photius also makes a distinction between acknowledging someone as a Father of the Church on the one hand and claiming that that person's teaching is flawless on the other.

It is through this distinction that Photius is able to make *his* claim on the Western Fathers of the Church, because he can allow that the Western Fathers may well have said things out of line with the truth of the Church and he can then say that their mistakes are to be treated with filial discretion. Thus, his implicit contrast to the Franks, who (he says) compound old dogmatic mistakes through their intransigence and injure fraternal relations by pitting the testimony of some Fathers against the testimony of other Fathers. In this way, Photius offers a refinement of the instincts we saw at work in Vincent's *Commonitory*: whereas Vincent clearly acknowledged that great teachers can make enormous mistakes, Photius is able to go further by saying that the great teachers are not necessarily compromised by making mistakes.

Photius also indicates in the *Mystagogy* how one ought to regard compromised teachers. Although he accepts that serious mistakes may be found in their writings, it is significant that he is prepared to accept that they nevertheless *are* Church Fathers. The idea that saints are perfect is intuitive and seductive and really rather silly. Photius' ability to acknowledge that theologians can make mistakes, even serious mistakes, and still be venerable, is commendable.

* * *

The examples that we have considered in this chapter, I suggest, are instructive for the attitudes that they demonstrated and the strategies that they employed in making sense of the earlier literature. They are far more important in this respect than they are as sources for definitive opinions about, say, Origen's relevance as a theologian, or what Gregory really meant, or whether Ambrose was right or wrong. From them, what we learn is that the transmission of the patristic heritage is based on a certain respect for the early teachers and fathers whose writings—or whose manner of life, for that matter—we are studying. This respect is not a fawning subservience. Instead, it is a product of the love that we share with them for God. This shared love infuses our relationship to them and thus motivates the desire (which was clearly announced by Vincent and Photius) to "cover the nakedness" of the Fathers.

In their practice, covering the nakedness of the Fathers is a way of responding to mistakes that is constructive and benevolent. Obviously, it is not an attempt at pretending that there are no mistakes to be found in patristic theology. It is, rather, an act of love that is motivated by regard for the dignity of a respected person. The respect is built up from the recognition that the person in question has dedicated a lifetime to serving God. It is implicitly an assertion that factors like that need to be considered when we are thinking about early theology. Since theology is, above all, a matter of responding to God and is a defining feature in how one lives, these factors surely matter.

But does it mean that, when we imitate Shem and Japheth in covering Noah's nakedness, we are saying that the Fathers made a mistake? A measure of confidence is required to respond in this way. And confidence has its place here, though it is not *self*-confidence, but a placing of faith in those who have gone before and even more importantly a placing of faith in God who joins us all together. What enables us to identify a mistake is discordance within the relationships that bind us to God and so to each other. Confidence rightly understood is an awareness of one's own place within those interconnecting relationships and a willingness to act within those networks. In other words, such confidence is informed by critical self-understanding.

Confidence of that sort is also apparent when we interpret the Fathers' writings theologically. There is a subtle but important difference between what Photius was doing and what Maximus was doing, and the distinction between judgment and interpretation helps to clarify this difference. Photius was in effect making a judgment about the value of certain theological claims; Maximus on the other hand offered an interpretation of a theological passage that was counter to another interpretation. Those exercises are similar because they are both evaluative, but if the difference between them is not appreciated we might get the wrong impression that Maximus was just trying to re-claim Gregory and so put him in the best possible light. In fact, even a casual reading of the *Ambigua* suffices to show that Maximus' engagement with Gregory's theology was very profound. What he was doing was more creative than simply contriving a way to show that Gregory was right all along. He was diving into the depths of Gregory's *Orations* with the assistance of techniques that he derived in part from Gregory himself. As a result, he offered a theological statement that spoke clearly to contemporary needs and that spoke in a patristic idiom. As we look back to what Maximus was doing, it is not too much to say that he was exemplifying the strategies of the Neo-Patristic Synthesis.

# *chapter three*
# SYMBOLS OF THE FAITH

So far, we have been considering what the patristic heritage is and the modes of its transmission. Along the way, in Chapter 1, we saw that we inherit from our forebears more than a set of interlocking propositions to which we give assent. In Chapter 2, we looked at the habits and practices that those forebears used to build up the heritage, in order to develop a sense for how we can participate in augmenting and transmitting it. These chapters have left to one side a major problem, however, which we will address directly in this chapter. Built up over dozens of generations, the heritage is vast and unwieldy—more than a single person over a whole lifetime could appropriate in its entirety, more even than a single community in a given time and place could adequately instantiate. Since we have taken seriously the warning that "Tradition" should not be treated anthropomorphically like a self-perpetuating and autonomous entity, we now need to think about how the patristic legacy can be managed and communicated by individuals. How can the vast legacy of Orthodox Christianity be rendered manageable?

In this chapter, we will think about how the content of that heritage is compressed in *symbols*, and expanded through interpreting those symbols. A symbol is easier to learn and to recollect than is the whole complex reality that the symbol represents. This means that, for our purposes, symbols are relevant because of their function. We will want to consider several of those functions. For instance, we will note how symbols can be used as tokens of membership: if you and I recognize a symbol, we have something in common. Thus, symbols play a role—in fact, a major role—in developing and maintaining identity within a given community. Another function is that, once we accept a symbol, it can serve as a node around which we organize and retain new information. Whatever isn't compatible with that symbol finds no ready place within one's expanding perspective. Both of these functions put me in mind of Hans-Georg Gadamer's laconic definition, "A symbol is something that facilitates recognition."[1]

After we have considered these themes and their implications, we will turn to several specific examples of symbols that are, or have been, meaningful for Orthodox Christians. In the following pages, we will explore some of those symbols in detail. But as we do so, our purpose is not to explain them exhaustively; it is not obvious that symbols can be exhaustively explained! Instead, we aim to understand better how patristic symbols are a major channel through which the influence of the Fathers is perpetuated. Exploring these themes will also help us identify problems that arise from confusing the ability to manipulate tokens of membership, on the one hand, with insight into what those tokens symbolize, on the other.

[1]Hans-Georg Gadamer, "Image and gesture," in *The Relevance of the Beautiful* (Cambridge, UK: Cambridge University Press, 1986), pp. 74–82 at p. 74.

## The symbol in antiquity and late antiquity

Our word *symbol* is a direct transliteration of the Greek σύμβολον. Long before that word circulated in the philosophical writings of Plato and Aristotle, it appeared in the historians and tragedians. There it describes an item—a knucklebone is a common example—that serves as proof of identity between people who have entered into some sort of contractual arrangement. The item is halved and each half is taken by one party. That the parties have claims on each other is verified by joining together the pieces (in Greek, the *symbola*). The practice of reuniting these pieces may explain the very origin of the word itself, since the noun σύμβολον appears to derive from the verb συμβάλλω, which means "to come together, unite" and by extension "to make a covenant." The device can be passed from one person to another, as when Herodotus describes the sons of a depositor coming to Sparta to reclaim the money and bringing *symbola* to establish their claim (*Histories* 6.86B). Not all arrangements involving these tokens or symbols were monetary: in Euripedes' *Medea*, Jason extends the hospitality of his friends to Medea and offers *symbola* to guarantee that she will receive it (lines 609–15).

This practice was well established enough that the term *symbolon* was detached from the piece of a sawn bone or broken coin to which it initially referred, and came to be attached to tokens of different kinds that served the same function. In the fifth century BC, the orator Lysias in his speech "On the property of Aristophanes" mentions a gold cup that is presented as a token from the king to indicate his willingness to underwrite a loan. Lysias calls the gold cup a *symbolum*. Likewise, in his play *Pseudolus*, the later Latin comic Plautus uses exactly the same word to refer to a piece of wax imprinted by a ring. This piece of wax identifies the Captain who has made a deposit for the purchase of a female slave and who will return later, with a "similar symbol" (*Pseudolus* 55ff.) and the balance, to claim her. Plautus lived during the third and second centuries BC; by the first century AD, Pliny the Younger referred to the signet ring itself as a "symbolum" (*Natural History* 33.4).

In these cases, the symbol in question acts to identify a person who has a specific relationship to another person. The symbol works as an identifier. A modern analogue is the renter's key to a safe deposit box, which can only be opened when two keys (the renter's and the guard's) are turned in the locks. But that analogy is imperfect because it leaves out something about the *symbolum* that received a great deal of attention from the ancients. The analogy would be closer if both the renter and the guard each had to produce their pieces of a single key and join them together before opening the box. This makes the analogy better because, unlike the key to a safe deposit box, the *symbolum* is a piece of a broken whole. For Plato and for Aristotle, it is exactly this incompleteness that is the symbol's most beguiling feature.

* * *

In a well-known section of the *Symposium*, Plato relates a myth offered by Socrates to account for love. According to this myth, humans were initially androgynous animals. These androgynous humans were circular, had eight limbs and, when they were in a hurry, they moved by stretching out their arms and legs and doing cartwheels (*Symposium* 189d–190a). But when they attempted to storm the heavens, Zeus split them in two and had Apollo turn their heads around so that they would see the wound and remember the consequences of their disobedience. (The navel is the point where the skin was stretched tight.) But humans despaired and so Zeus installed in them love and this prompted a desire to identify and to be restored to the other half of oneself: "Love is born into every human being; it calls back the halves of our original nature together; it tries to make one out of two and heal the wound of human nature."[2] It is at this point that the word *symbolon* comes into the myth, for Socrates claims that "each of us, then, is a 'matching half' [σύμβολον] of a human whole, because each was sliced like a flatfish, two out of one, and each of us is always seeking the half that matches him."[3]

The yearning that the *symbolon* feels for its matching half is taken up by Aristotle (fourth century BC). In Book Seven of his *Eudemian Ethics*, Aristotle discusses friendship. This leads him to ponder love and the appropriate end of loving desire. Aristotle writes,

> But in a way love of the opposite is also love of the good. For opposites strive to reach one another through the middle point, for they strive after each other as *symbola*, because in that way one middle thing results from the two. Hence accidentally love of the good is love of the opposite, but essentially it is love of the middle, for opposites do not strive to reach one another but the middle.[4]

Aristotle's distinction between love of the opposite and love of the middle recalls the Socratic myth of the first, androgynous human.

[2]Plato, *Symposium* 191d; trans. Alexander Nehamas and Paul Woodruff (Indianapolis, IN: Hackett, 1989).

[3]Ibid.

[4]Aristotle, *Eudemian Ethics* 1239b30–35; trans. H. Rackham (Cambridge, MA: Harvard University Press, 1952).

But Aristotle goes further. It is true that love attracts opposites, but this is only true with respect to the accidents of the case (i.e., when we consider the particulars of each lover separately). What is essentially true about loving attraction, according to Aristotle, is that it brings the lovers together in a relationship of love that is the "middle." Love brings two complementary things together to form a whole.

The images offered by Plato and by Aristotle are very vivid. They draw our attention to something that is easily missed: a symbol yearns for completion. It doesn't just demurely hint at some other thing. It really desires to be rejoined to what it symbolizes. But this means that the presence of a symbol always attests to an absence—the absence of that which it symbolizes. A symbol functions precisely because it is a fragment that harks back to the fragmented whole. The brokenness of the symbol is an imperfection, but this is not an impediment to the symbol's function; as Gadamer said rightly, "the imperfection of a symbol is not a shortcoming but the other side of the work of abstraction that it performs."[5] The imperfection of a symbol is necessary for its function. In other words, the defining characteristic of a symbol is that it is incomplete, and its incompleteness calls attention to what is missing. This is what James A. Coulter has called "the suggestive incompleteness or hinting power of the symbol."[6]

Rather than looking further into the use of this key term in ancient and late ancient hermeneutic theories, we need to assess two factors evident in the early sources that we have surveyed. The first

[5]Hans-Georg Gadamer, *Truth and Method*, second, revised edition (New York: Continuum, 1989), pp. 346–47.

[6]James A. Coulter, *The Literary Microcosm* (Leiden: Brill, 1976), p. 61.

function of a symbol is for identification. This is an overtly social function. In some cases, we can specify its social role: it can be financial or commercial, or it can have to do with the rites of hospitality. Even in later authors, who were deeply committed to interpreting literary "symbols," there is still a social dimension to the symbol, but we will come to that in due course. First, we need to recall how a literary identification of symbols grew naturally out of the symbol's social function. Because the process of identification by a symbol is in the first instance a matter of joining together two broken pieces to form a whole, symbols have a secondary function. They allude to that which is absent, thus representing the whole of which they are a part.

A symbol evokes what is absent. Because that is what a symbol does, even when it succeeds in some way in making present that which is absent, the symbol still underscores the fact of the other's absence. But because the symbol attests to something that is absent, the connection between the symbol and the symbolized can be tenuous, even arbitrary. This potential problem is compounded in cases of ancient symbols, since over time their original reference can be displaced entirely by new associations.

## Symbols in early Christianity

Early Christians used the word "symbol" and its cognates just as their contemporaries did. It could refer to something as seemingly simple as a token, a marker the meaning of which could serve to identify Christians. Or a symbol could be something as relatively complex as an abstract representation of non-material realities. Christian artwork provides many examples. Christians also considered some forms of words to be symbols—verbal symbols, as it were. In this case, too, Christians knew of the basic social functions that a symbol could perform. There is also evidence coming from an unexpected quarter that they were also aware of symbols' power to suggest what is absent. We will take some of these ideas in turn. In doing so, we will have occasion to see how early Christians adapted classical uses and understandings of symbols and how, in doing so, they built up the church. Afterward, we can take stock of how ancient Christian symbols continue to resonate within Orthodox Christianity.

* * *

First, then, consider a symbolic token. Christians identified the *fish* as a symbol for Christ. Clement of Alexandria, for example, endorses the fish (among other symbols) as an appropriate image for Christian signet rings (*Paedagogus* 3.11). There are many examples of miracles in the New Testament that involved fish, any of which might have prompted the association. But what seems to have made the fish especially suitable was the fact that the Greek word for fish (ἰχθύς) could be taken as the acronym for the Greek "Jesus Christ, God's Son, Savior" (Ἰησοῦς Χριστός, Θεοῦ Υἱός, Σωτήρ). Oddly, that sequence of words—followed by the word "cross"—appears in an oration that Eusebius appends to his *Life of Constantine*, called Constantine's "Oration to the assembly of saints." In the oration (ch. 18), Constantine identifies those words as an acrostic from a poem by the Erythrean Sybil. The same acronym may have motivated Tertullian, who knew Greek, to call Christians "little fish, after the image of our *ichthys*, Jesus Christ" (*On baptism* 1).

In addition to these references in literature, we have evidence for the symbolic fish in sculptures and relief carvings. The "Jesus fish," familiar to us from bumper stickers and baseball caps, is based on this symbol. But unlike its modern abstract and highly stylized form, ancient examples are often naturalistic. There were, however, stylized depictions of the symbol that didn't remotely resemble fish and that were based instead on the Greek characters of the word. This depiction of the symbol is an eight-spoked "*ichthys*-wheel":

This symbol is achieved by overlapping the five Greek characters ΙΧΘΥΣ (with the horizontal bars of the iota, Ι, and of the sigma, Σ, being curved). Here, the Greek letters are traced in black:

This playful rendering of letters into a monogram is not entirely unique from the early period. The Chi-Rho (from the first two letters of the Greek word *Christos*) is as well known as the *ichthys*-wheel. A widespread opinion holds that these symbols enabled Christians to identify one another during the early persecutions. That may be so. Certainly, ancient uses of symbols as identity markers make it an undeniable possibility. Or maybe Christians were simply glad to have an abstract symbol that represented their beliefs.

What we have seen already indicates how ideograms are enmeshed in complex verbal systems. Some early Christian symbols did not rely on ideograms at all, but rather were verbal constructions that functioned at a much higher level of abstraction. Canon Seven of the fourth-century Council of Laodicaea indicates that symbols must be "thoroughly learned" by certain heretics before they can be admitted to communion. A similar expression is found in the sixth-century *Corpus Iuris Civilis*, a compendium of legal texts that re-established the Roman Empire on an explicitly Christian foundation. In one passage, the word "symbol" glosses the expression "the holy teaching" (*Codex Justinianus* 1.1.7.11). These symbols are *creedal formulae* that distinguish orthodoxy from heresy. Bearing in mind the two major functions of symbols that we have just established, we note of these symbols *both* that they are densely coded statements referring to highly complex beliefs *and* that their affirmation is an integral part of joining the communion of the orthodox.

It is not brevity and simplicity as such that make these statements symbols, since some of them are long and feature technical terms. As "symbols," these creeds are relatively concise statements of holy teachings that point beyond themselves to a greater reality of which the creed is but a part. The creed is not complete and self-sufficient. It is not a vessel that contains the truth; it is a signpost that directs us truly. The character of a creed is that it is suggestive, rather than exhaustive. As a "symbol of the faith," a creed does not fully explicate Christian teaching once and for all, but there is an even more important sense in which the creed is (to use Gadamer's word) "imperfect." The creed is not for that reason morally or ontologically flawed, since the imperfection is a structural feature that enables the creed to do what it is supposed to do.

In effect, this incompleteness allows space for the words of the creed to express their yearning. Like all symbols, creeds strive for completeness. This completeness comes from our enacting the creed—not just reciting its words, but impressing them into the very substance of our lives. It is through impressing the creed into our lives that the creed is justified in its ability to designate membership within the society that affirms it. The creedal symbol fills itself out by structuring the outlook and, thus, the manner of living of the believer. Its structure orients the believer's activity by providing and identifying stable landmarks that describe a pathway for living. It is, so to speak, at the terminus of this pathway that the creedal symbol finds its completeness, for here the yearning of the creed is satisfied in God.

* * *

But of course the creed does not actually fill itself out. Rather, *we* interpret and elaborate upon it; we "unpack" it. We do so chiefly by directing attention to key phrases in it. It is in making sense of these phrases that matters become exceptionally complicated, because at this point the interpretation of dense symbols and the social functioning of symbols interact in significant ways. Take the formula "three persons, one nature." This formula is a concise expression of Orthodox belief regarding the Trinity: three persons equally instantiating a single nature. There is great value in such a concise expression, but it needs to be noted that there is a serious (and, as it happens, a very ancient) temptation to regard that expression as obligatory. By that, I mean that many people have been—and some still are—tempted to think that conclusions can be drawn from the mere absence or presence of that expression. The lazy approach to this symbol, and others like it, is that if it is present, all's well; if it isn't, there are problems. This approach (mis)informs the way we make sense of ancient writings. Instead of patiently learning from them and allowing this reading to re-work and enrich our expectations, we take key phrases (often derived we know not from where) and assert that they are *the* criteria such that their presence or absence in effect determines how to interpret the document in question.

The problem isn't the use of shorthand or otherwise inadequate concepts in a preliminary, unrefined attempt at understanding. So long as we are prepared to refine our concepts instead of holding stubbornly to them, there is no reason to be embarrassed by or ashamed of inadequate early efforts. They are heuristic devices doing their job by helping us to ask questions and to integrate the answers we get; they are prejudices in the sense of being ini-tial judgments, rather than being resolutely unanalyzed biases. Where the problem enters is when we go to the evidence looking to have our views confirmed, rather than to learn from that evi-dence, come what may. If we are resistant to learning in this way, what is impaired is the "dialectic" or "openness" of understand-ing (to retrieve other terms from Gadamer's *Truth and Method*). We grow in our understanding of the riches of the past when we are open to the challenges posed by the witness of the past, not when we amass a huge fund of ancient trivia in support of our own perspective.

This temptation is not limited to academics interpreting ancient documents. It is a living concern whenever a formula is taken as a litmus test for the rightness or wrongness of someone's beliefs. A particularly good example comes from the word *homoousios*, an adjective meaning "*of the same substance* or *stuff*" according to Lampe's *Patristic Greek Lexicon* (or, more woodenly, "same-in-being"). The word describes the commonality of the Father and the Son as one God. Thus Origen, in his comments on Psalm 54.4: "the Son of the Father, the consubstantial (*homoousios*) king, though 'taking the form of a slave' (cf. Philem 2.7)." In this comment, the word *homoousios* goes directly against the belief that Christ is a composite being who is therefore different in being from the Father, and the underlying theological belief that there is a difference in being between the Father and the Son. It was for this reason that the word was used in the Nicene Creed. Athanasius used it frequently in his many writings against Arian Christology, and also in the first of his *Letters to Serapion* to make explicit the belief that the Spirit, too, was "of the same stuff" as the Father. At each stage, the word was as contentious as was the theological position for which it was the emblem: not all Christians have always believed that the Father, the Son and the Spirit are equally one in a single divine being.

Like Athanasius, Gregory the Theologian was a great proponent of employing the word *homoousios* to the Spirit no less than to the Father and to the Son. So it was an awkward matter for him that Basil the Great was reserved in his writings about asserting the full divinity of the Spirit. Gregory attributed this reservation to Basil's sense of the consequences that would ensue if he were to provoke his opponents at a critical juncture:

> He postponed for the time the use of the exact term, begging as a favour from the Spirit Himself and his earnest champions, that they would not be annoyed at his economy, nor, by clinging to a single expression, ruin the whole cause, from an uncompromising temper, at a crisis when religion was in

peril. He assured them that they would suffer no injury from a slight change in their expressions, and from teaching the same truth in other terms.[7]

Gregory goes on to say that Basil did indeed "adore the Spirit as consubstantial and coequal with the Father and the Son" and that the fruits of this adoration were manifest in Basil's actions and writings. But he also stipulates that he wants "to prevent men from thinking that the terms found in his writings are the utmost limit of the truth, and so have their faith weakened, and consider that their own error is supported by his theology" in that Basil avoided a term which subsequently became an integral part of the profession of orthodox faith. What Gregory thinks Basil's readers ought to do instead is to "[consider] the sense of his writings, and the object with which they were written, so as to be brought closer to the truth, and enabled to silence the partisans of impiety."[8]

Gregory's point is not that words are irrelevant. Words are tremendously important. That is exactly why he expended so much effort trying to ensure that the consubstantiality of the Spirit with the Father and with the Son would be accepted. Gregory's point, rather, is that words and their meanings are not lifeless abstractions that can be separated from their usage. The significance does not inhere in a few linked syllables, or even in a run of words conforming to an expected pattern. It mattered for Gregory that Basil's life indicated his affirmation of the full divinity of the Spirit precisely because the meaning of Basil's teaching is not restricted to Basil's words. What Gregory was claiming was that Basil's

---

[7]Gregory Nazianzus, *Oration* 43.68; trans. NPNF, second series, vol. 7, p. 418.

[8]Gregory Nazianzus, *Oration* 43.69; NPNF, II: 7, pp. 418–19.

avoidance of the word *homoousios* is nothing like as important as the fact that his life exemplified his belief in the full divinity of the Holy Spirit. "For our salvation," as Gregory says, "is not so much a matter of words as of actions."[9]

These extracts, taken from Gregory's funeral oration for Basil, illustrate some important points about what we are to make of symbolic language. Throughout this section of his oration, Gregory insists that the symbols of the faith—such as the term *homoousios*—are not always and in all places obligatory. Basil, Gregory claims, was right to exercise discretion, lest "by clinging to a single expression," he "ruin the whole cause, from an uncompromising temper." At the same time, Basil's discretion does not exempt us from using the proper terms at the right times: we must not think that "the terms found in his writings are the utmost limit of the truth."[10] We need to be ready to build on what Basil wrote and did, to carry forward his legacy, and to emulate his manner of living. But as we do those things, we cannot live as though Basil was the last word in Christian theology. As for Gregory, his oration emphasizes that the symbolic word *homoousios* is important because it reinforces the understanding of Christian salvation and thus shapes the practice of Christian living.

*  *  *

Before moving on to our next topic, we need to note one final application of the language of symbols. Or rather, we need to note a case where that language is sharply restricted by the Fathers. We have seen that a symbol is suggestive, that in its imperfection

[9]Gregory Nazianzus, *Oration* 43.68; NPNF, II: 7, p. 418.

[10]Gregory Nazianzus, *Oration* 43.69; NPNF, II: 7, p. 419.

it points beyond itself. These characteristics define and therefore limit what count as symbols. We have seen how an ideogram is a symbol, and how a creed is a symbol, because their incompleteness suggests something beyond themselves. Because symbols function in this way, we do not refer to the Eucharistic gifts as the "symbol" of the Body of Christ. Indeed, that is why some ancient Christians expressly insisted that such language must *not* be used. In the fourth book of his *On the Orthodox Faith*, St John of Damascus (eighth century) devotes several pages to discussing the sacrament of the Eucharist. He explicitly rejects the claim that the consecrated bread and wine are symbols:

> The bread and the wine are not merely figures of the body and blood of Christ (God forbid!) but the deified body of the Lord itself: for the Lord has said, "This is My body," not, this is a figure of My body: and "My blood," not, a figure of My blood. And on a previous occasion He had said to the Jews, "Except ye eat the flesh of the Son of Man and drink His blood, ye have no life in you. For My flesh is meat indeed and My blood is drink indeed. And again, He that eateth Me, shall live."[11]

As so often, the Damascene was not striking out on an uncharted path. He was reiterating, consolidating, and developing a well-known teaching here. A similar position had already been advanced in the fifth century by Theodore of Mopsuestia, when in the fragments of his comments on the Gospel he remarks that the Lord said at Matthew 26.26, "This is my body" and did *not* say, "This is the symbol of my body."

---

[11]John of Damascus, *On the Orthodox Faith* 4.13, citing Jn 6.51–55; trans. NPNF, second series, vol. 9, p. 83.

The language of imperfection, which is implicit when we talk about symbols, is entirely out of place in this context. The Eucharistic gifts are not an ontologically defective substitution or intermediary for God whose presence they "symbolize." Taken in that way, the Eucharist gifts might mediate between God and humans, but by occupying a position between them they would also attest to the distance between them. The Eucharist is more than a device to elicit memories of Christ. But most importantly—and here is where the vast difference between the symbol and the Eucharist becomes clear—the Eucharist does not attest to Christ's absence. Rather, it celebrates Christ's *presence*. There is a sufficiency in the Eucharist that is entirely different from the restlessness of the outward trajectory of symbols. This is not to deny the importance of symbols, nor is it to claim that there are similarities in the ways that symbols do what they do and the way that the Eucharist does what it does. Instead, insisting that the Eucharist is not a symbol of Christ's body and blood, because the limitations inherent in symbols do not apply to the Eucharist, is a way of taking symbols seriously and using symbols responsibly.

## Ancient symbols and modern communities

Symbols have tremendous longevity. They are stable, however, because they are dynamic. Over time, a symbol can accommodate multiple referents and can be interpreted variously. To give a trivial example, because it has been a prominent symbol for centuries, a rose is never simply a rose. Symbols change, and it is no surprise that symbols from antiquity that we continue to use can well mean different things now than they meant when they were initially formed. This may be a matter of an original, but minor, theme coming to prominence. It may be a matter of new connections that are suggested when a symbol is translated into a new culture or language. These are ways in which the content can be augmented or supplemented. There are also negative changes. It may be a matter of old references falling into disuse, or even being deliberately suppressed. These mutations do not change the shape of the symbol. In that sense, they are internal to the symbols by altering its reference (rather than its appearance). They could also be seen as *relative* because they concern how the symbols relate to the referents that they symbolize. But the symbol itself remains unchanged.

The durability of symbols enables them to identify, not merely individuals, but entire communities. The compact that a symbol represents—something that, with Herodotus, Euripides, or Lysias, was formed between small groups—can just as easily be opened up to define membership within a community. This is the expanded social function of symbols. Symbols can be recognized by many people whose mutual recognition of a given symbol creates a bond between them. Gadamer has similarly assessed the role played by symbols in establishing group identity: "A congregation understands its symbols and finds confirmation of itself in that recognition."[12] Christians exploited this function of symbols when they articulated symbols of faith. We have already seen this process at work when we reflected on the expectation of the council Fathers at Laodicaea that, before heretics can be received into the Church's communion, they must have learned the "symbols."

[12]Hans-Georg Gadamer, "Aesthetic and religious experience," in *The Relevance of the Beautiful*, pp. 140–54 at p. 150.

Symbols grow and develop over time along with the populations to which they belong (and which they promote), and the symbols we have been studying have developed within a very sophisticated society and are among the key features of that society that have been retained or recalled over time. From their origin, then, these symbols implicate and are implicated in a web of historical conventions and attitudes that grew up within a particular population. They are markers of membership that have been refined over long centuries. It is for that reason that recitation of the Creed can suffice to bring specific Christians from certain backgrounds fully into the Orthodox Church. By subscribing to the Creed, they are brought into the fold. In general, less is required for entry into the Orthodox Church by those whose background is meaningfully similar to the Orthodox ethos; more is required of those whose background is foreign to that ethos. For some, what is expected is the profession of the Orthodox faith; for others, it may be chrismation; for still others, catechism and baptism. But all these entry points are symbolic thresholds.

Of course, there is more to ancient symbols in Orthodoxy than thresholds. They certainly are not peripheral to the experience of Orthodox Christians, as a fence or a hedge is to a field. Symbols are pervasive in Orthodox life. We might even say that they furnish Orthodoxy. They are the features whose presence and position relative to each other characterize Orthodox Christianity. The symbols themselves are resilient, though again this stability is dynamic in that the symbols can survive considerable modification with respect to their referents. This means that, although symbols are a stabilizing feature, they are not in themselves resistant to change—nor could they be without ossifying and so losing their ability to function properly! And so, despite the initial appearances to the contrary, they are not necessarily politically or ideologically conservative.

What they conserve is not some social *status quo*, but the apparatus for introducing people into the fellowship of Orthodox Christians on pilgrimage to God. It is within this configuration of symbols that we hear echoes, even if sometimes only mutedly, of an entire course of historical experience. Symbols do not function in isolation from the particularities of that experience. They attest to the relationship within time that joins the eternal and infinite Holy Trinity to those temporal and limited creatures who are called to be saints. They direct our aspirations toward God. In this way, symbols serve to build up Orthodox culture, which for all its variegation is basically a human conversation with God.

But precisely because symbols function as cultural tools in this way, it is possible and appropriate to scrutinize their historical character and to think critically about their usefulness. (These are tasks that any good training in the discipline of historical theology equips scholars to undertake.) Thinking critically about their use does not mean thinking negatively, or denying their value as tools. It is no more an insult to think critically about our conceptual tools than it is to decide that a framing hammer is the wrong thing to use to break up concrete, or that it would be a good idea to use a chisel instead of ruining the screwdriver.

* * *

Keeping in mind what we have already considered about symbols, let's come back to the Nicene-Constantinopolitan Creed. Now we will focus on the implications of thinking of it as a symbol with respect to the different versions of that Creed that are in use in different communities. The choice of this Creed in particular is motivated because, under several aspects, it can be considered as the symbol *par excellence*. As the Fathers of the Council of Chalcedon (451) affirmed,

> This is the faith of the orthodox. This we all believe. In this we were baptized, in this we baptize. [ . . . ] This is the true faith. This is the holy faith. This is the eternal faith. Into this we were baptized, into this we baptize. We all believe accordingly.[13]

Another reason we will focus on the Nicene-Constantinopolitan Creed is because it has come down in two forms, and the difference between them (which has been the topic of intense controversies for centuries) presents an extremely interesting case for us to think about the Creed as an ancient symbol with a long and complex history.

From its inception, the Creed served as the focal point for theological differentiation. It is well suited to that purpose, because it is replete with precise theological terms and, in its earliest form, culminated with a series of denunciations aimed at Arius and his supporters. Long custom makes the genuine oddity of reciting this creed liturgically less than obvious. But a comparison to a creed prominently used liturgically in the Christian West—the Apostles' Creed—suffices to indicate how technical the Nicene-Constantinopolitan Creed is.

The longest article by far in the Apostles' Creed is a chain of affirmations about Jesus Christ that are taken almost entirely from the New Testament, the exception being the clause "He

---

[13]*Acts of the Council of Chalcedon*, Session II, §11; trans. R. Price and M. Gaddis (Liverpool: Liverpool University Press, 2006), vol. 2, p. 12.

descended into hell" (which is a theme from extra-biblical sources). The affirmations about the Father and the Holy Spirit are very brief indeed. The confession of God does not invoke theological terminology. The final articles of the Apostles' Creed affirm belief in "the holy catholic Church, the communion of saints, the forgiveness of sins, the resurrection of the body, and the life everlasting." By contrast, the Nicene-Constantinopolitan Creed employs several analogies and a scattering of technical vocabulary to describe how Jesus Christ relates to God the Father. Like the Apostles' Creed, it affirms the forgiveness of sins but only by way of describing the "one baptism" that is its principal affirmation. Perhaps the only instance where the Apostles' Creed is more theologically precise than the Nicene-Constantinopolitan Creed is in its affirmation of "the resurrection of the body," where the Nicene-Constantinopolitan Creed anticipates "the resurrection of the dead," something slightly more general.

It is neither necessary nor desirable to conjecture why the Creeds differ in these respects. It is enough, having noted them, to appreciate how relatively dense and relatively theological (so to speak) the Nicene-Constantinopolitan Creed is. The characteristic density of theological expression in the Nicene-Constantinopolitan Creed is a deliberate feature that recalls the origin of the Creed in a council that gathered to resolve theological controversies. The Councils of Nicaea and of Constantinople were convened to quell debates, especially debates about how Christ's relationship to God the Father is to be understood, and the Symbol of the Faith is a concise expression of their teaching. So what has been carried over into weekly (if not daily) usage in the Byzantine liturgical tradition is a statement that is Christologically precise in its attempt to differentiate correct belief from erroneous belief.

This symbol contrasts an orthodox mindset with heresy, which makes it a powerful device for generating and sustaining cohesion within the fellowship of believers. As the only creedal statement in regular usage, this symbol has great significance. The sharp reaction by the Fathers of the Fifth Ecumenical Council (Constantinople, 553) to the "impious creed" of Theodore of Mopsuestia, which was read out toward the end of the fourth session, underlines the point: "This creed was composed by Satan. Anathema to the writer of this creed! This creed together with its author was anathematized by the First Council of Ephesus. We recognize only one creed, that which the holy fathers of Nicaea issued and transmitted . . ."[14] The great significance attributed to the Nicene-Constantinopolitan Creed means that any divergence, particularly in the form of the Creed as it is recited in any other group, will make an enormous impact. Hence, the intense interest in the western profession that the Spirit processes from the Father *and the Son*, a topic that has generated a great deal of theological heat, and sometimes even a bit of light, for centuries.

We need to work our way through here carefully. Putting to one side the question of the Holy Spirit's procession, we need to consider how the level and kind of attention devoted to the word *Filioque* compounds any theological difference that the presence of the word as such might disclose. The two major functions of the symbol—first, as a token of identity; second, as an incomplete witness to a greater whole—are conflated in this case, with the result that the difficulty of addressing the theological difference is compounded. Since the two functions are not sufficiently distinguished, a difference in the token of identity is taken to indicate

[14]*Acts of the Council of Constantinople of 553*, Session IV, §82; trans. R. Price (Liverpool: Liverpool University Press, 2006), vol. 1, p. 270.

that the two forms actually attest to different understandings of the Trinity. And perhaps they do. But this is a conclusion to be established, not an axiom to be asserted.

Distinctions of function have been obscured in part as a result of a general shift from regarding the Creed as an authoritative expression of truth about God, to considering it the definitive text. To see that this is so, we will first survey the developments that have tended to support the idea, crucial to polemical theology, that the precise wording of the Creed is of the utmost importance. Next, we will note that not all divergences in various versions of the Creed are taken to be objectionable. Finally we will look at evidence that, even within the Byzantine tradition of the Orthodox Church, the Creed has been treated, with all respect, as a document that does in fact admit of further articulation.

Once again, it is not my purpose to adjudicate in the matter of the *Filioque* as a contested issue in Orthodox-Catholic relations. Instead, I want to draw attention to the functional ambivalence of the Creed, which has allowed subsequent generations to treat it either as a foundation for further contemplation, or as a landmark for tactical maneuvers in inter-confessional conflict.

* * *

It is a matter of longstanding convention for Orthodox theologians and jurists to take the presence in the Creed of the *Filioque* as violating a sacrosanct text. This opinion is based on a common reading of the seventh canon of the Council of Ephesus. As we saw in Chapter 2, that canon made it illicit for anyone "to bring forward, or to write, or to compose a different Faith as a rival to" the creed of Nicaea. This sentence has been taken to make the wording of the Creed inalterable, and so to make any theological modification of the document especially odious.

One cannot help being reminded of an observation from the anthropologist Mary Douglas: "It is only by exaggerating the difference between within and without, above and below, male and female, with and against, that a semblance of order is created."[15] Perhaps attention to the *Filioque* exaggerates the difference between the Byzantines and their heirs on the one hand and the Latins and their heirs on the other, so as to create a semblance of order. The suspicion that something odd is going on in this particular case is bolstered when we find that other discrepancies between versions of the Creed are let pass without comment. I say "versions of the Creed" here because there survive not only the Latin and the Greek received texts, but also Armenian and Syriac texts. No two are completely identical, even allowing for the exigencies of translation. The Syriac and Armenian versions are not without interest—we have already noted that a Syriac version of the creed says that the Spirit is "from the Father and the Son," for instance—but for simplicity, we will focus here on the Latin and Greek discrepancies.

If maintaining the purity of a text is what matters (as clearly it does when the precision of a symbol as an identifier is at stake), then it is surely strange that no one seems bothered that the received Latin version describes the Son as "God from God (*Deum ex Deo*), Light from Light, True God from God," whereas the received Greek version has only "Light from Light, True God from True God." It is not clear why this variation is tolerated.

[15]Mary Douglas, *Purity and Danger: An Analysis of the Concepts of Pollution and Taboo* (London: Routledge and Kegan Paul, 1966), p. 4.

Another divergence that seems not to offend is the difference between the Latin "I believe" and the Greek "We believe." That difference is not so readily apparent because modern Orthodox practice is to recite the verbs in the Creed in the first person singular ("I believe . . . I acknowledge . . . I await"). But this practice in itself amounts to a divergence, since the Creed was originally set down in the plural ("We believe . . . we acknowledge . . . we await")—as it was read out on October 10, 451 during the second session of the Council of Chalcedon. To my knowledge, no Orthodox polemicist comments on this divergence, which is not surprising, since it would be difficult to insist on the inviolate purity of the text as recited in modern Orthodox liturgies (with its singular verbs), while simultaneously acknowledging ancient evidence that the Creed was recited with plural verbs. All of this is to say nothing about divergences that arise in vernacular translations. For instance, regarding the Incarnation the Latin text says, *homo factus est*. If translated "He was made man" (as it often is, in my experience) rather than "He became man," a Latin expression that is grammatically ambiguous becomes an English expression that is unmistakably different from the only possible English translation of the parallel Greek text.[16]

---

[16]The translation "He was made man" supposes that the infinitive form of the verb *factus est* is *facere*, which is grammatically defensible. But the infinitive *fieri* ("to become")—a deponent verb in its own right that is often used as the passive form for the verb *facere*—is an equally grammatically defensible possibility. It also corresponds more closely with the Greek verb in the parallel clause, ἐνανθρωπήσαντα, which is the singular masculine accusative form of the active aorist participle from ἐνανθρωπέω (and which therefore *cannot* be passive). On the basis of the Greek parallel, one could argue robustly that the English translation "He was made man" misconstrues the underlying Latin, which should be presumed to be consistent with the Greek in default of a compelling argument to the contrary.

What these points illustrate is that, with respect to the Creed, divergence as such seems not to be as problematic as perceived *theological* divergence is. This indicates that what matters is the faith in God that the Creed symbolizes, rather than the precise configuration of the Creed as a symbol. So why do we perceive some changes to the symbol to be theologically significant, and others to be innocuous? Why is it that the clause "and from the Son" is so threatening, but the other differences are not?

There is a great deal of evidence that the *Filioque* is merely one of many causes for the estrangement of eastern and western Christianity, and not necessarily a particularly important one at that. In *The Byzantine Lists,* Tia Kolbaba has identified and studied a series of polemical writings. In the process, her book shows that many of the errors endlessly catalogued by Byzantine controversialists were examples of xenophobia, scandal-mongering or party-politicking.[17] In historical perspective, the *Filioque* is the great survivor, a clod of mud that stuck. It was also the only major theological difference to appear regularly in those lists. That the *Filioque* has survived the great winnowing process of history does not, however, in itself determine how theologically serious it actually is (which is a question that I will not address here). Rather, the conditions under which the *Filioque* took on such importance suggest that there are other things at stake here than theological accuracy. As the other items from the catalogues of errors fell into disuse, the *Filioque* became all the more important in maintaining the symbolic boundary between the Christian east and the

[17]Tia Kolbaba, *The Byzantine Lists: Errors of the Latins* (Champaign, IL: University of Illinois Press, 2000); See also Prof. Kolbaba's *Inventing Latin Heretics: Byzantines and the Filioque in the Ninth Century* (Kalamazoo, MI: Medieval Institute Publications, Western Michigan University, 2008).

Christian west. Its role as the sole theological difference goes a long way toward explaining why the problem of the *Filioque* is so difficult to redress. That problem will remain intractable, I suspect, for as long as the Creed *as a form of identity* and the Creed *as a witness to God* are not distinguished in principle.

* * *

What is needed for a respectable response to this dilemma? A first step, I suggest, is to distinguish the Symbol's role as a boundary marker from its role as a signifier of something greater than itself. One step that can be taken in that direction is to accept that the Nicene-Constantinopolitan Creed, for all its importance, is actually not the only legitimate creed in Christendom. Excerpts from several councils quoted in this chapter amply attest to the pre-eminence of the Nicene-Constantinopolitan Creed, but the acts of the very same councils also demonstrate unexpected subtlety regarding how the council Fathers understood the creed issued at Nicaea, clarified at Constantinople, and received at Ephesus and elsewhere. To acknowledge explicitly that there are multiple genuine creeds is not to prejudice the questions raised by the *Filioque*. What it accomplishes instead is to divest some of the associations that we as Orthodox have toward that Creed simply because it is the Creed that we overwhelmingly tend to use. If we were to acknowledge that other ancient creeds do not propose "another faith rival to" that of the Nicene Creed, we could then reflect seriously upon the Nicene-Constantinopolitan Creed as the symbol of the faith rather than as guarantor of the faith.

In practical terms, this could take the form of accepting that other Christians affirm their faith through the Apostles' Creed (and, until relatively recently, the Athanasian Creed) and that, throughout

Christian history, there have been many more creeds that have legitimately expressed tenets of Christian belief. Mention can be made of the baptismal creed in the *Apostolic Tradition*, the two forms of a Creed mentioned by St Cyril of Jerusalem in his *Catechetical Homilies*, Epiphanius of Salamis' variant of the Creed and his enlarged, interpretive version of the Creed (both of which his *Ancoratus* preserves), and the baptismal Creed of Antioch as related in St John Cassian's *On the Incarnation*, among many others.

It might be argued that some of these examples should be understood in fact simply as commentaries on the Nicene-Constantinopolitan Creed, particularly since some of them are too convoluted and ungainly to be suited for liturgical recitation, but that argument assumes that a creed needs to be a document for liturgical use. It is far from obvious that this is the case. More important than the appropriateness for liturgy are the formal and thematic features common to Christian creeds. Some of the obvious features are an affirmation of belief in God, in Jesus Christ as a historical man who was also God's Son, in the Holy Spirit, in the church, and in the resurrection.

Awareness of the Nicene-Constantinopolitan Creed's place—which is generally agreed to be a privileged place—amongst these other creeds that proliferated before and after it will help us recalibrate our ideas about what the Creed does. What I would call a "purist" attitude toward the very words of the Creed makes the social function of this particular symbol all-important. The success of the Symbol of the Faith in establishing group identity, when coupled with the belief that the group is right by definition, creates a strong presumption that anyone who does not endorse the symbol (and so is not a member of the group) must therefore be wrong. But if we pay attention to the proliferation of creeds in the history of Christianity, we will notice very quickly that forming social groups is only the most basic function that the Creed serves, and we will see that the Creed functions in other ways as well. In addition to creating and maintaining social boundaries, the Creed also works as a symbol to orient and to ground our yearning toward the Trinity and thus to promote further theological reflection. The way that the Fathers of the Council of Chalcedon responded to the Creed can guide our thinking in this matter.

The second session of the Council of Chalcedon was advised that the "question now to be investigated, judged and studied is how to confirm the true faith."[18] What makes their deliberations relevant to our topic is that they immediately responded to the chairman, the patrician Anatolius, "No one makes a new exposition, nor do we attempt or presume to do so. For it was the Fathers who taught, what they expounded is preserved in writing, and we cannot go beyond it."[19] They endorsed the spirit of the Fathers of Ephesus, as evident in the Second Canon's prohibition.

But they could not be content with a mere reading of the old Creed from Nicaea or the Nicene Creed as modified at Constantinople: they had assembled to redress controversies that had grown up after the Creed and that took the Creed for granted. In fact, the most outspoken proponent of going no further than the Nicene Creed was none other than Dioscorus of Alexandria,[20] the bishop condemned at Chalcedon. Dioscorus was, in this regard at least,

---

[18]*Acts of the Council*, Session II, §2; trans. Price and Gaddis, vol. 2, p. 10.

[19]*Acts of the Council*, Session II, §3; trans. Price and Gaddis, vol. 2, p. 10.

[20]See *Acts of the Council*, Session I, §§141–48; trans. Price and Gaddis, vol. 1, pp. 154–55.

much the most conservative hierarch in attendance. In effect, he called down the judgment of the Fathers upon anyone who would dare to augment the Creed: "Let each person express his opinion in writing: can we enquire or revise in addition to this Creed? If anyone has instituted an inquiry that goes beyond what has been said, ordained and decreed, will he not rightly incur the sentence of the Fathers?"[21]

"The sentence of the Fathers" that Dioscorus invokes is, as it happens, an imperfect citation of Canon Seven from Ephesus. Since the other hierarchs had also echoed that canon, they might seem to be in an awkward position. Dioscorus' conservatism is simple: nothing is permitted to go "beyond what has been said, ordained and decreed." Without explicitly rejecting that claim, the council Fathers instead put forward additional documents to ensure that the Creed is interpreted correctly: the Tome of Leo, as well as Cyril's second letter to Nestorius and letter to John of Antioch. After those documents were read out, the council Fathers proclaimed:

> This is the faith of the fathers. This is the faith of the apostles. We all believe accordingly. We orthodox believe accordingly. Anathema to him who does not believe accordingly! Peter has uttered this through Leo. The apostles taught accordingly. Leo taught piously and truly. Cyril taught accordingly. Eternal is the memory of Cyril. Leo and Cyril taught the same. Leo and Cyril taught accordingly. Anathema to him who does not believe accordingly! This is the true faith. We orthodox believe accordingly. This is the faith of the Fathers.[22]

[21]*Acts of the Council*, Session I, §943a; trans. Price and Gaddis, vol. 1, p. 340.

[22]*Acts of the Council*, Session II, §23; trans. Price and Gaddis, vol. 2, pp. 24–25.

Then they accused Dioscorus of obscuring earlier discussions elsewhere, by omitting reference to these documents. Clearly, they were not intimidated by Dioscorus' appeal to the canon from the Council of Ephesus!

The council Fathers reflected on what they had done in the definition of the Council of Chalcedon. They reaffirmed the prohibition from Ephesus, while making clear that the Constantinopolitan version of the Nicene Creed was accepted on a par with the Nicene Creed itself. They also specified the Creed's exclusive usage for purposes of converting "to the knowledge of the truth" pagans, Jews, or heretics. But at the same time they obviously considered it legitimate to provide additional exposition of the faith as it is symbolized in the Creed when that faith is jeopardized.[23] Not only did they cite the letters of Cyril and the Tome of Leo, they even appended their own theological definitions—advanced boldly as the deliberations of "this holy, great and ecumenical council now present."[24] All of these teachings are harmonious, and it is this harmony that demonstrates how the later expositions and elucidations are *not* violating the Creed. To borrow a phrase from St Maximus the Confessor, they are the Fathers' "further interpretations and detailed explanations" instead of the "poor understandings and misinterpretations" offered by others.[25]

The interpretive apparatus that has been installed over the centuries by the Fathers of Chalcedon and others is instructive.

[23]*Acts of the Council*, Session V, §34; trans. Price and Gaddis, vol. 2, pp. 203–5.

[24]Ibid.

[25]See Maximus the Confessor, *Opuscula polemica et theologica* 21; *Patrologia Graeca*, vol. 91, col. 260.

Although the Creed was recognized at Chalcedon as serving as the uniquely appropriate affirmation that should be made by those joining the community, it was not treated as a self-sufficient and comprehensive document. The option of treating in that way was put forward by Dioscorus and decisively rejected by the council Fathers who instead promoted a tradition of explication by centering the Creed within a network of other statements.

As for the *Filioque*, these considerations have not prejudiced any outcome to discussing the specific questions that it prompts. They are merely a lesson in the historical course of the Creed, over a fairly limited period. The *Filioque* is not a factor in the period we have been considering. It has however been a fixture for many centuries since, and it cannot be brushed away, despite the proposal from some quarters (for instance, by western delegates to the Bonn Conference of 1874 and 1875) that it should be abandoned in the interests of ecumenical dialogue. Those who espouse the clause understand it as a theological elucidation that is compatible with earlier theological elucidations and consistent with a specific theological tradition. We have looked at many examples of theological elucidation—even referred to a few cases of creeds based on the Nicene-Constantinopolitan Creed—and on that basis can accept that expositions of the Creed are not in principle illegitimate. Whether it is theologically accurate, and whether it is a valid interpolation are different questions that remain.

Entertaining those questions is beyond the scope of this chapter. What we have seen, however, is that the Creed is not regarded as a self-interpreting, exhaustive, and final statement of the faith. Commenting on it is not precluded. Its existence does not arrest theological expression or preclude theological development. It is not, and does not pretend to be, the last word. It is a symbol that initiates people into the community of the faithful, sustaining them as they grow in the faith. As such, conversation about it should not be arrested by too great an emphasis on the symbolic boundaries that the Creed generates, for this would abridge the Creed's authentic ability to elicit our aspirations toward fuller understanding.

* * *

This chapter has been dedicated to the roles that patristic symbols play in Orthodox Christianity, with special attention to the Nicene-Constantinopolitan Creed as the preeminent symbol. We have commented on the two basic functions of a symbol—that it allows for recognition and thus has a social dimension, and that it intimates what is absent and yearns for completeness. Symbols are not univocal. A single symbol can suggest many things, though a good symbol will not suggest too many (since, if it did, it would be useless). I have suggested that the functional incompleteness of symbols enables them to survive a gradual, if in some cases continuous, degree of transformation. Symbols are dynamic through the activity of referring to other things, and this dynamism accounts for how symbols endure, even thrive, over time. It also makes them especially valuable vehicles for transmitting culture.

Symbols have the potential to grow as we grow. They incorporate us into the fellowship of Christians and train our aspirations. They are quintessentially more than the sum of their parts. "In the case of the symbol," Gadamer wrote, "[ . . . ] the particular represents itself as a fragment of being that promises to complete and make whole whatever corresponds to it. Or, indeed, the symbol is that other fragment that has always been sought in order to complete and make whole our own fragmentary lives."[26]

After thinking about those topics, we considered some ways in which ancient Christian thinking is misunderstood. The case of the word *homoousios* was discussed. The word is beyond question important to the articulation of Orthodox Christology and, over time, it has come to symbolize the Orthodox position in contrast to several heretical positions. But because the word has become a symbol, we can be tempted to think that it is a characteristic marker for Orthodoxy. It is not. It is possible to be Orthodox without using the word, as Basil the Great was (much to Gregory the Theologian's chagrin). And it is also possible to use the word without being Orthodox. The mere presence or absence of a term is inconclusive, no matter how much symbolic charge that term has. As Gregory taught in his funeral oration for Basil, a life that is in accord with the full divinity of the Holy Spirit is more important than a word on the lips. Since Basil manifested the divinity of the Holy Spirit in his life, his life itself pointed to—we might even say symbolized—the truth of the word *homoousios*.

We then moved on to the more complex case of creeds understood as *symbola*. Given their prominent role in initiating new members into the community, the social function of the Creed is easy to spot. And considering the eschatological orientation of creeds, they are readily recognized as devices that point beyond themselves to an anticipated completion. Our survey of the discussions on the Creed at the Council of Chalcedon reinforced the point that symbols are incomplete. Both of these findings suggest that

[26]Hans-Georg Gadamer, "The relevance of the beautiful," in *The Relevance of the Beautiful* (Cambridge, UK: Cambridge University Press, 1986), pp. 2–53 at p. 32.

conservative preoccupation with the Nicene-Constantinopolitan Creed can be problematic.

Symbols are restrictive only in a very trivial sense. True, they establish some boundaries—as definitions will do—but they go on to inspire, to suggest unanticipated links. That is, they provide structure within which we are able to grow. They are rather like the walls of a building. The thing to remember, though, is that symbols are the walls of the house that we inhabit, not the prison that restrains us. We are not trapped by them. And we do well to remember, too, that the Lord described himself in these words: "I am the door: by me if any man enter in, he shall be saved, and shall go in and out, and find pasture" (Jn 10.9).

*chapter four*

# FORWARD WITH
# THE FATHERS

In the first chapter of this book, we looked at the alleged contrast between two schools of thought in recent Russian Orthodoxy: Russian religious philosophy on the one hand, and the
neo-patristic synthesis on the other. These schools are in some
ways exemplified in the persons of Fr Sergius Bulgakov and Fr
Georges Florovsky, respectively. It was suggested that one way of
appreciating their difference is to think that religious philosophers
like Bulgakov went "beyond the Fathers," whereas patrologists
like Florovsky went "back to the Fathers." Although that differentiation has much to recommend it, we found it to be not entirely
satisfactory. Bulgakov was well aware of how his work was built
on the foundation of patristic theology; Florovsky was well aware
of how his work was more than an archaeological undertaking.
So I suggested as a refinement to the earlier schematization that,
when Orthodox theologians go "back to the Fathers," they do so
in order to move *forward* with the Fathers.

The second chapter of this book presented several case studies.
These studies had in common the topic of patristic reactions to
patristic theology, or how the Fathers read the Fathers. From these

examples, we began to work out a rudimentary theory of theology as a historical discipline. In the third chapter, we turned our attention to another phenomenon. Here, our subject was the elaboration of a network of symbols from the patristic era. These symbols taken together constitute an important vehicle for the transmission of Orthodox culture, not least by providing the framework within which we are able to understand the ancient heritage of Orthodox theology. Together, these two chapters gave an account of the methods and modes by which ancient theology has been propagated down the centuries. In the final chapter of this book, we are going to turn our attention to patristic theology in modern Orthodoxy.

The first thing to be considered under that heading is the limitation of patristic theology. We will take as an example the debates that surround the theology of John Zizioulas, Metropolitan of Pergamon. These debates focus on the question of how to regard the modern theological appropriation of ancient theological writings. Is such an activity nothing more than the statement of an ancient message in a contemporary idiom, the recapitulation of timeless verities? Is it a misrepresentation, or an abuse, of historical material? (Some critics who think that Zizioulas' theology is a misrepresentation actually denounce it as a heresy.) Is it a tacit admission that Orthodox theology can speak only in the dialect of late ancient Greek or Church Slavonic? Addressing these questions will contribute to our understanding of the place of patristic theology in modern Orthodoxy.

The second section of this chapter will make the case that recourse to ancient theology enables us to engage critically with the modern world. That is, a thorough knowledge of patristics equips the modern Orthodox Christian with a range of values—even a worldview—that can be used to identify, assess, and criticize the conventional beliefs and values of our society. In this way, the patristic heritage can embolden us to articulate a Christian vision for the world, instead of accepting supinely whatever values our society happens to endorse. By this point, we have seen that simply stating the received opinions of Eastern European Christianity is not adequate; still less is it adequate to repeat those received opinions in a louder voice if it seems that they are being ignored. Instead of falling back into a closed community to preserve its inheritance (or, alternatively, to insist that the only possibility to engage with other people is if they join that community and accept its terms and language), we have seen that the Orthodox heritage is sufficiently rich and open-ended that we can use it to interact with society.

The third and final topic in this chapter will build upon the first two sections by presenting examples of how patristic writings can provide a basis for more than just doctrinal reflection. Theological doctrine does not exhaust the patristic heritage. Here, we will consider ways in which patristic writings can inspire theologically informed responses to practical and social concerns. Some themes in St John Chrysostom's writings, for example, help us see how patristics can motivate us to respond to modern problems about economics and social justice. We can start to see how the Fathers provide us with tremendous resources for rising to the challenges of contemporary life.

## The limitations of patristic theology

In the English-speaking world, the pre-eminent living Orthodox systematic theologian is Metropolitan John (Zizioulas) of

Pergamon. His reputation is based on his many years as professor of theology in the University of Glasgow and as visiting professor in Kings College London, but also on his influential and much-discussed book *Being as Communion*.[1] A major theme in that book, and in other publications, is Zizioulas' argument that *being* is expressed in persons and that the fullness of being is to be sought in free relationships between persons. To use technical language, Zizioulas has posited a *relational ontology*. This may seem forbiddingly abstract, but what Zizioulas offers is a theologically driven response to modern crises that stem from individualism. In other words, Zizioulas responds to problems that come from tending to think of the *individual* (with all the connotations of that term: rugged, free, probably selfish, possibly narcissistic) as the primary unit of experience and reality. Zizioulas sees this, rightly, as an impoverished concept of human reality. In contrast with that concept, Zizioulas insists that the primary unit of reality is the Trinity. The Trinity is the paradigm of free and full communion, to which we humans have access through Christ—most intimately, through Eucharistic participation in the body and blood of Christ within the communion of the Church. In this way, Zizioulas embeds his critique of individualism and his counter-project in theological and ecclesiastical language.

One might disagree with Zizioulas' account of individualism or even his account of the Church, but for our purposes we can put those hypothetical disagreements aside. What is relevant for us is another problem, namely that Zizioulas presents his theological work as nothing other than a modern exposition of classical Greek theology as found especially in the writings of the Cappa-

---

[1] John Zizioulas, *Being as Communion: Studies in Personhood and the Church* (Crestwood, NY: St Vladimir's Seminary Press, 1985).

docian Fathers. We can take a good example from the introductory chapter to *Being as Communion*, where Zizioulas claims straightforwardly,

> This ontology, which came out of the eucharistic experience of the Church, guided the Fathers in working out their doctrine of the being of God, a doctrine formulated above all by Athanasius of Alexandria and the Cappadocian Fathers, Basil the Great, Gregory of Nazianzus and Gregory of Nyssa.[2]

Later, he goes on to argue that Basil the Great seems to have been "rather unhappy with the notion of substance as an ontological category and tends to replace it—significantly enough for our subject here—with that of κοινωνία [i.e., communion]."[3] With reference to Basil's *On the Holy Spirit* 18, Zizioulas even asserts that "communion is for Basil an ontological category." These examples showcase how quickly Zizioulas shuttles between developing his relational ontology as a modern theological project and offering his exposition of doctrines chiefly from the fourth century.

Alongside these recurring references to the Greek Fathers, there are also in Zizioulas's book frequent references to modern thinkers. Zizioulas does not attempt to disguise the extent to which his work is in conversation with writings by Martin Buber, Emmanuel Levinas, and Wolfhart Pannenberg, to name but a few.[4] To the contrary, he deliberately casts his theology in an idiom that resonates with contemporary philosophy and theology. In effect,

[2]Zizioulas, *Being as Communion*, p. 17.

[3]Ibid., p. 134.

[4]See ibid., pp. 17, 44–46 n. 40, 78 n. 41.

Zizioulas' writings presume that there is no contradiction between a theological study being written in a modern idiom and it simultaneously being an exposition of ancient theology. In brief, it is Zizioulas' contention that his ecclesial and relational ontology of personhood is a statement in modern language of the teaching of the Fathers of the Orthodox Church.

* * *

That contention has been challenged on several fronts. Here, we are going to focus on only one of the challenges to Zizioulas' theology, leveled most clearly by Lucian Turcescu.[5] This criticism is relevant to our study because it draws attention to underlying methodological questions about the retrieval, or even the redeployment, of patristic insights in modern theology. Turcescu acknowledges Zizioulas' "concept of person" as "a meaningful and seemingly coherent concept, showing his interest in modern issues and his attempts to use ancient insights to address them."[6] And yet Turcescu accuses Zizioulas of attempting to "foist on the Cappadocian Fathers" contemporary philosophical insights into personhood.[7] Turcescu draws attention to several examples of ambiguity, particularly in the writings of St Gregory of Nyssa, which challenge Zizioulas' claim to have drawn out the meaning of Cappadocian theology. Let's take a specific example.

Turcescu points out that Gregory is by no means reluctant to use the word "individual" (in Greek, ἄτομος). Indeed, Turcescu cites one passage by Gregory in which he equates the words "indi-

[5]Lucian Turcescu, "'Person' versus 'Individual', and Other Modern Misreadings of Gregory of Nyssa," *Modern Theology* 18 (2002): 527–39.

[6]Ibid., p. 528.

[7]Ibid., p. 528, cf. p. 536.

vidual" and "person" (πρόσωπον). He identifies other passages where Gregory uses the word *hypostasis* (ὑπόστασις, a technical theological term usually translated in English as "person") and "individual" interchangeably.[8] Philological arguments sometimes seem obscure or irrelevant, but Turcescu's point is quite simple: he argues from this evidence that Zizioulas' sharp distinction between the "person" and the "individual" is not native to Gregory's thinking, and that Zizioulas' interpretation imposes upon ancient documents categories that are foreign to them, indeed that are anachronistic.

Turcescu goes on to speculate on possible modern influences on Zizioulas,[9] from which it is suggested Zizioulas derives the categories that are applied to interpreting (or are "foisted on," to use Turcescu's terms) Cappadocian theology. Turcescu's case appears to be that Zizioulas' interpretation of the Cappadocians is misleading because it attempts to simplify features of their writings that were inoffensive at the time, but that now seem loose and potentially confusing.

It is not necessary here to adjudicate between Zizioulas and Turcescu, or to assess other critiques of Zizioulas' reading of the Cappadocians.[10] Our interest in the debates about Zizioulas is the

[8]Ibid., pp. 533–34.

[9]Ibid., pp. 534–36.

[10]The most noteworthy critiques are by André de Halleux; see his " 'Hypostase' et 'Personne' dans la formation du dogme trinitaire (ca. 375–81)," *Revue d'histoire ecclésiastique* 79 (1984): 313–69, 625–70 and "Personalisme ou essentialisme trinitaire chez le Pères cappadociens? Une mauvaise controversie," *Revue théologique de Louvain* 17 (1986): 129–55, 265–92. See also Demetrios Bathrellos, "Church, Eucharist, Bishop: The Early Church in the Ecclesiology of John Zizioulas," in Douglas Knight, ed., *The Theology of John*

light these debates shed on method in historical theology. Simply put, we want to know about the use that Zizioulas makes of ancient theological writings, and we want to think about how others have responded to it. We begin with an observation made by Aristotle Papanikolaou in responding to Turcescu's critique. Papanikolaou says that Zizioulas has identified the "core of theology" from reading the Fathers and is attempting (in full awareness of the contemporary relevance of these issues) to re-state that "core" in a modern idiom.[11] Papanikolaou then argues that the criticism of Zizioulas supposes that there are only two options for theologically engaging with patristic literature. The first is to read that literature without any prior beliefs whatever, lest these beliefs interfere with the meaning of the literature; the second is a largely mechanical repetition of patristic formulae. Papanikolaou writes:

> He [Zizioulas] is no more superimposing a philosophical system on the Eastern patristic writers than did these same writers Hellenize the teachings of Jesus. His attempt to give further expression to the realism of divine-human communion through twentieth-century notions of person is analogous to the patristic co-opting of Greek philosophical categories to express the same principle. Zizioulas is doing exactly what these writers did insofar as he is thinking about

*Zizioulas: Personhood and the Church* (Aldershot: Ashgate, 2007), chap. 8; Alan Brown, "On the Criticism of *Being as Communion* in Anglophone Orthodox Theology," in Knight, *The Theology of John Zizioulas*, chap. 2; and Aristotle Papanikolaou, "Is John Zizioulas an Existentialist in Disguise? Response to Lucian Turcescu," *Modern Theology* 20 (2004): 601–7.

[11]Papanikolaou, "Is John Zizioulas an Existentialist in Disguise?," pp. 603–4.

the authoritative texts of the tradition in light of the questions, challenges, and prevailing philosophical currents of his time. The alternative is either the hermeneutically impossible bracketing of all that the interpreter has read and experienced as they approach the patristic texts in the hope of distilling the pure "essence" of the text itself; or to judge contemporary Orthodox theology as authentic based on its faithful reiteration of patristic texts, i.e., a form of patristic fundamentalism. The latter, however, is not consistent with the approach of the patristic writers themselves, who did more than simply reiterate their predecessors.[12]

As we have seen in Chapter 2, there is abundant evidence to corroborate Papanikolaou's claim that there were patristic writers who "did more than simply reiterate their predecessors." St Maximus the Confessor's engagement with the theology of St Gregory of Nazianzus is a fine example. There are passages in *Ambigua* that can fairly be described as the "updating" of traditional theology. By that token, what Papanikolaou is claiming for Zizioulas is the Christian freedom that the Fathers themselves enjoyed in the business of articulating their good news in the idiom of their contemporaries.

* * *

In *Communion and Otherness*,[13] Zizioulas himself takes up the challenge that his critics have made against him. He does not redress the hermeneutic-*cum*-historical problem that

[12]Ibid., p. 605.

[13]John Zizioulas, *Communion and Otherness: Further Studies in Personhood and the Church*, edited by Paul McPartlan (London and New York: T & T Clark, 2006).

Papanikolaou identified, which is an opportunity sadly lost. Instead, he presents his theological writings as a simple restatement of Cappadocian theology, above all as read through the writings of Maximus the Confessor. Zizioulas provocatively asserts that answering Turcescu's criticism "would appear to any student of theology as defending the obvious."[14] What is at stake for Zizioulas (and, apparently, for Turcescu and others) is the substantial accuracy or otherwise of Zizioulas' theological assertions.

But even a reader sympathetic to Zizioulas' theology should admit that there are basic questions here that require attention. For example, startling as it may be to ask, why does it matter whether or not Zizioulas is faithfully representing the theology of Basil and of Gregory of Nazianzus? Both Zizioulas and Turcescu attribute to the Fathers great importance. But neither of them is critical in making that attribution; that is, there is no evidence in their writings that they have reflected in a sustained way on the nature and extent of the importance of patristic theology. The reader is left to conclude that the Fathers are important in a maximal, but unspecified, way. Their meaning, if not their precise vocabulary, is considered self-evidently and entirely sufficient and so Zizioulas' theology can be authenticated by determining if its content (the "core of theology," to echo Papanikolaou) is identical to the content of patristic theology. But how can that determination be made?

By responding to Turcescu's criticism with a dismissive remark, Zizioulas neglected to take the opportunity to clarify his thinking about the historical ways of theology and thus to explain how we can recognize identical theological content in different modes of

[14]Ibid., p. 171.

expression. Papanikolaou's response to Turcescu moves toward answering that question, raising for explicit consideration the dynamics of "thinking about the authoritative texts of the tradition in light of the questions, challenges, and prevailing philosophical currents" of our time.

Though they are permeated with classical Orthodox patristic terms, even citations, *Being and Communion* and *Communion and Otherness* were not written for the guild of patrologists; instead they have been offered up for general theological consideration. In this way, they strive to go beyond what Papanikolaou calls "patristic fundamentalism" and what Alan Brown similarly calls "patristicism."[15] Papanikolaou does not elaborate on what he means by "patristic fundamentalism" but Brown is expansive about "patristicism," which consists in the attempt to install a scholarly tradition (described in some detail by Brown) as being "absolutely normative for Orthodox theology."[16] What is involved is the attempt to constrain the expression of Orthodox theology to modes, terms, and forms that are patristic—or anyway that are *thought to be* patristic. That stipulation needs to be made because, sometimes, these constraints are derived less from the historic course of the patristic heritage than from a particular configuration of beliefs that merely gives the impression of antiquity. In such cases, what is received from time out of memory (even if it is time only just barely out of living memory) is taken as a genuinely ancient and stable feature of Orthodox Christianity. Regardless of the pedigree of these beliefs, what really matters is that they are asserted to be the criteria for recognizing what is Orthodox.

[15]Brown, "On the Criticism of *Being as Communion*," pp. 64, 76.

[16]Ibid., p. 77.

This mentality poses a much more serious danger for recourse to patristic culture than does the vague misgiving that late ancient theology is probably not relevant in the modern world. Allegations of irrelevance might initially ring resoundingly, but the deeper we enter into the study of Christian antiquity the fainter those allegations echo in our ears. The same is not true of the attitude that seeks to make boundaries out of patristic resources. This attitude can become stronger the deeper we enter into studying ancient Christianity, because that study produces more resources that can then be used to build walls (for example, between "traditional" Christians on the one hand and "rootless" Christians on the other). The danger here is that unexamined motivations direct the process of studying ancient sources, privilege certain terms (without necessarily understanding them), and unjustly restrict Orthodox theology to a particular idiom (namely, the idiom of patristic theology as reconstructed by modern theologians). It is unjust for the inheritance from the ancient church to be employed to reinforce complacency, pride, or nostalgia; it is unjust for study to be subordinated to a self-serving agenda. If any of those things happens, our access to the historical transmission of Christian truth comes to be curtailed. For example, if we allow modern politics of communal identity to determine the course of our study of Christian antiquity, we will have a powerful motivation to ignore features within the historical evidence that are unserviceable, embarrassing, or otherwise untidy with respect to identity politics. Any such commitment is misguided. It keeps before our eyes an artificial image of the past that is perfectly unchanging because it is totally lifeless.

Ironically, there is an important sense in which Zizioulas' appeal to the theology of the ancient Fathers oddly reasserts that patristic theology is the limiting case for modern theology. No doubt, Zizioulas' recourse to the language and ideas of contemporary philosophy means that he cannot be accused of patristic fundamentalism, in that his use of existentialist and kindred philosophical terminology is out of line with the fundamentalist approach. Even so, Zizioulas' lack of clarity about historical theology poses a problem. The way that he appeals to St Basil or to St Maximus suggests very strongly that patristic theology is normative. Meanwhile, his curt rebuttal of Turcescu's criticism seems to indicate that systematic theology is a straightforward translation of the core content of patristic theology (per Papanikolaou) into merely a different theological idiom. Zizioulas appears to make patristic theology the touchstone for theology as such. This appearance is corroborated by Zizioulas' unwillingness to be seen as anything other than a contemporary commentator drawing out the meaning of ancient theology. This posture leaves him open to criticism from scholars unconvinced that his theological writings are defensible as historical commentaries. On the other hand, if Zizioulas' arguments are accepted, his theological writings are presented simply as the re-statement of patristic truth in a contemporary idiom.

What seems to be left out is the possibility of a re-deployment of patristic themes that are justified with reference to something other than their own venerable antiquity. One way forward, surely, is to say simply and straightforwardly that theology is valid and authentic not by virtue of its relationship to earlier theology, but rather by virtue of the witness it bears to God and the salvation worked by God for creation. What is *not* necessary is to claim that all theology is patristic theology.

* * *

Throughout this review of the debates about John Zizioulas' theology, I have declined from taking a position about the value of his theological writings or the historical accuracy of his claims about the theological writings of the Cappadocians and Maximus the Confessor. It is not that these questions are meaningless. But even more important than the discussion of what contributions patristic study can make to systematic theology is the question of methodology. In this survey, I suggested that Zizioulas attempts to access the "core" of patristic theology with no further ado. To attempt such a thing is necessarily problematic, and the lack of attention to how such a thing can and should be done gives us pause.

It is difficult to accept that Zizioulas' contributions to systematic theology are neither more nor less than a repackaging in contemporary terms of the content of the primary theological insight of the Greek Christian tradition. This is simply because there is no attempt at explaining how meaning can exist stably across history despite the changing forms of that meaning. The impression given by Zizioulas' writings is that, despite his philosophically-sophisticated engagement with ancient themes and terms, he regards patristic theology as an endlessly malleable, but ever constant, substance that can be shaped into formations that are different in appearance but identical in content. But doesn't this imply that only what can be traced back to the Fathers is theologically legitimate? Or, using a different metaphor, doesn't it make the Fathers' writings into boundary markers beyond which theology does not go, for fear of jeopardizing its legitimacy?

## Despoiling the Egyptians

The way John Zizioulas draws on the early Christian heritage is worth so much of our attention because his writings claim to be substantially identical to the message of the ancient Fathers. Even as Zizioulas has sought to bring the riches of the Orthodox inheritance to modern systematic theology, he has insisted that his writings are basically a recapitulation of ancient theology in a modern idiom. This points to an underdeveloped aspect of Zizioulas' theology—namely, its relative neglect of the historicity of Orthodox doctrine.

Zizioulas is by no means unique in trying to authenticate his theological claims by claiming that they are identical to ancient theology, which is presumed to be preeminent. But every case of this type presents a problem. In the absence of a clear case for patristic theology being not just historically prior but essentially identical to all valid modern theology, the only thing we are given is a preference for the cultural history of Orthodox Christendom and its accomplishments. That isn't to say that there is no way to defend such a preference. But we have to acknowledge that it is not self-evident that such a preference should be universal.

It is one thing to have doubts about whether people who are not native heirs to Orthodox cultural history would be enthusiastic for the ways of patristic theology. But above and beyond that, we can be sure that uncritical invocation of the Fathers to legitimate current practices causes dissatisfaction within Orthodox culture itself. A choice specimen of this critical reflection is in the story "A Brief Tale about the Antichrist," published over a century ago in *Three Conversations* by Vladimir Soloviev (1853–1900).[17]

[17]A recent, annotated translation of "A Brief Tale of the Antichrist" is in V. S. Soloviev, *Politics, Laws, and Morality: Essays*, edited and translated

* * *

In Soloviev's story, three fictional conversations are hosted by an anonymous Lady in her salon in Switzerland; they are attended by the General, the Politician, the Prince, and Mr. Z. The first three take it in turn to present their own theses, which the others then discuss. The final contributor to the proceedings is Mr. Z. It is generally agreed that Mr. Z's contribution represents Soloviev's own views. At the invitation of the Lady, Mr. Z reads "A Brief Tale about the Antichrist" written by a certain Fr Pansophius of the Danilov Monastery. What Fr Pansophius offers, and Mr. Z then relates, is a cautionary tale about the seduction of political power that dresses itself in the trappings of Christianity.

The story is compulsively readable, but resists easy summary. The main interest for us is the critique of Orthodox attitudes toward antiquity. We encounter this in a passage where Mr. Z relates the temptations the Great Man (as the Antichrist is called) puts before Catholic Christians, then Orthodox Christians, and then Protestant Christians in his bid to be recognized as the Divine Majesty in the flesh. To the Catholics, the Great Man offers to confirm and re-establish the political authority of the Papacy as outlined in a medieval forgery known as the Constantinian Donation, which purported to be Emperor Constantine's grant of temporal power to the Pope. To the Protestants, the Great Man offers to establish a "World Institute for the Free Investigation of Holy Scripture," thus appealing to a quasi-idolatrous infatuation with the Bible and an unexamined confidence in the reasoning powers of the mind. The Great Man's offer to the Orthodox (who by this time

by Vladimir Wozniuk (New Haven, CT: Yale University Press, 2000), pp. 264–89.

have been reconciled with the Old Believers) is better quoted than paraphrased:

> Dear brethren! I know that among you there are those for whom the most precious things in Christianity are its *sacred tradition*, ancient symbols, hymns and prayers, icons and ceremonial service. And in fact, what can be more valuable than this for the religious disposition? You know, My beloved, that today I have signed a law directing large sums of money to the World Museum of Christian Archeology in Our glorious Imperial City Constantinople, with the aim of collecting, studying, and preserving all relics of church antiquity, especially of the Eastern Church. And I ask that tomorrow you select from amongst yourselves a commission to discuss with Me those measures which should be taken with the aim of drawing the contemporary way of life, morals, and customs closer to the tradition and ordinances of the Holy Orthodox Church! Orthodox brethren! Whosoever finds My Will in his heart, whosoever can call Me his heartfelt true Leader and Lord, let him come up here.[18]

Over half of the Orthodox Christians, including hierarchs, monks, and laity, join the Great Man on his imperial dais. The Catholic and Protestant delegations had fared similarly.

In this passage, Soloviev's story dramatizes the congenital weaknesses of the Christian confessions. According to the story, the great problem for Orthodox Christians is an obsessive interest in historical details (hence, the tempting institution is an archeological museum), especially the trappings of religious devotion (hence, the emphasis on prayers, hymns, and icons—and, tellingly, the

[18]Soloviev, "A Brief Tale of the Antichrist," p. 280; emphasis in the original.

total lack of emphasis on teaching and studious reflection, which in Soloviev's tale tempts Protestant rather than Orthodox Christians), and the desire to impose "the tradition and ordinances of the Holy Orthodox Church" upon "contemporary way of life, morals, and customs" (which is no doubt a pointed comment on the conservative tendency of the Byzantine "symphony" of Church and State).

Soloviev's anxiety about coercion in matters of social and ethical life is part of his vision for Christian politics, which is a rich and complex topic that cannot detain us here. But even setting that topic aside, we are left with a pen portrait that sharply criticizes the presumption that the relics of the past are intrinsically important and that they therefore ought to be observed, if not cherished. Soloviev implies, probably rightly, that such an attitude is widespread amongst Orthodox Christians. Perhaps the presence of this attitude explains the habit of depicting modern Orthodoxy as a simple restatement in modern language of ancient Orthodoxy. But that disposition toward the past is most definitely not universal.

Consider another cautionary tale, this one written by Soloviev's older contemporary, Nathaniel Hawthorne (1804–1864). Hawthorne's parable "The Earth's Holocaust" relates how the people of America assemble in the Great Plains for a kind of apocalyptic spring-cleaning. They intend to rid themselves of "warn-out trumperies . . . by a general bonfire."[19] The energetic clearing away of old rubbish becomes a binge of frantic destruction: first the waste of society, then its hindrances and indignities, but finally

[19]Nathaniel Hawthorne, "The Earth's Holocaust," in his *Mosses from an Old Manse*, vol. II (Boston and New York: Houghton Mifflin and Company, 1900), pp. 195–228, at p. 195.

its very triumphs and substance, are consigned to a blazing pyre that eventually draws to itself the inhabitants of the entire world, who likewise pile their offerings on to the flames. Hawthorne's narrator watches the spectacle with growing alarm, then horror. The tipping point seems to be around the time that the fire is fed on books:

> "See! see! what heaps of books and pamphlets!" cried a fellow, who did not seem to be a lover of literature. "Now we shall have a glorious blaze!" "That's just the thing," said a modern philosopher. "Now we shall get rid of the weight of dead men's thought, which has hitherto pressed so heavily on the living intellect that it has been incompetent to any effectual self-exertion. Well done, my lads! Into the fire with them! Now you are enlightening the world, indeed!"[20]

What motivated the massive bonfire in Hawthorne's story was, in the first instance, an enthusiastic sense for the potential held out by the present. This enthusiasm embraced a growing number of people who only had in common a vigorous desire to see something burned to ashes, on grounds that the thing to be destroyed has been holding people back. There are a few descriptions of recidivists. The drunks who filched a bottle of booze that rolled out of the flames; the staunch conservative whose only comfort is the firm expectation that, after he has been flung by liberals into the flames, they will assuredly throw themselves in next; the inconsolable bookworm ("one of those men who are born to gnaw dead thoughts . . . covered with the dust of libraries"):[21] all of these people stand aside pathetically.

[20]Hawthorne, "The Earth's Holocaust," pp. 214–15.

[21]Ibid., p. 219.

In this nightmarish vision, enlightenment comes, not from the books, but from the flames that destroy them. The paradox comes from naïve and uncritical confidence that the unencumbered exercise of the mind will be self-sufficient. The frenzy of destruction is driven by uncritical ideas about freedom. It hardly needs to be said that freedom is at a premium in our society. And the sense of frustration with the past is only likely to be sharper in a consumer society stocked with merchandise that is designed to be obsolete (or at least replaced) within a matter of months. The suggestion that the past is deadweight is not easily shrugged off. Given the prevalence of this attitude in the modern world, it cannot be assumed that the public at large will share the enthusiasm for the ancient legacy of Christianity that motivated most of the Orthodox in Soloviev's story to join the Great Man.

* * *

What Hawthorne's modern philosopher celebrates, and what Soloviev's Antichrist used to seduce the Orthodox, are two sides of the same coin. Despite that difference in attitude toward the past as related by the two storytellers, in the end the characters in both Hawthorne's and Soloviev's stories seem to regard the legacy of culture as an inert deposit within the historical landscape, like it or loathe it. What the authors portray are two divergent ways of responding to cultural history in its concrete expressions, both of which are in the end horribly destructive.

The problem that both visions share is their assumption that the historical legacy is fixed and closed. A glimmer of optimism near the end of Hawthorne's story underlines the point. The narrator, despairing that even Bibles have been consigned to the flames and so anticipating that the following day nothing will be left "better or worse than a heap of embers and ashes," is comforted:

> I beheld among the wallowing flames a copy of the Holy Scriptures, the pages of which, instead of being blackened into tinder, only assumed a more dazzling whiteness as the finger-marks of human imperfection were purified away. Certain marginal notes and commentaries, it is true, yielded to the intensity of the fiery test, but without detriment to the smallest syllable that had flamed from the pen of inspiration.[22]

Human imperfections, in the form of marginalia and commentaries, are purged by the flames, leaving behind simply the inspired content of Holy Scriptures. There is, in this vision as in Soloviev's, precious little scope for acknowledging the value of contributions that subsequent generations have made to propagating holiness. Hawthorne's Puritan idealization of the (fire-retardant) Bible is the analogue to Soloviev's Orthodox idealization of sacred antiquities, although Soloviev's attitude is more subversive.

By subverting the strong desire on the part of some Orthodox to impose ancient culture on the present, Soloviev also challenges the instinct of some modern Orthodox to identify the exposition of patristic writings as the only legitimate vehicle for theology. An important thing that the attitude criticized by Soloviev overlooks in the patristic writings is the extent to which the ancient Fathers of the Church were receptive to the intellectual culture in which they lived. By their time, there was already awareness of the apostolic tradition and of how to cultivate it (as St Irenaeus of Lyons, c.130–200, had made clear in his *Refutation of All Heresies* and

[22]Ibid., p. 225.

*Demonstration of the Apostolic Preaching*). But this awareness did not lead most early Christians to think that the tradition is a feeble thing to be protected from contact with the world around it that might contaminate it; it did not generate a widespread tendency to sectarian thinking.

Early examples of articulating the Christian faith in a way that would be culturally informed (rather than purist in isolation) return to a particular episode from biblical history: the "despoiling of the Egyptians." On three occasions, it is mentioned that the children of Israel—especially the women—were supposed to borrow gold, silver, and fine clothing from their Egyptian neighbors before departing for the promised land (Ex 3.22, 11.2, 12.35–36). The next time these treasures are mentioned, as the Christian exegetes duly noted, was when Moses collected gold, silver, brass, precious clothes and woods, and dyed skins from the people to create a sanctuary for God to dwell in their midst and to furnish it with the appurtenances of religious worship (Ex 25.1–8, 35.4–29, 36.3–7). Significantly, sanctuary and its furnishings were patterned after a heavenly exemplar that God revealed to Moses (Ex 25.9, 26.30, 39.32; Acts 7.44; Heb 8.5). The connection discerned by the Christians between these events was that Egyptian gold was used in the fashioning of the tabernacle.

The perceived connection was stated clearly by Origen of Alexandria in a famous letter to St Gregory Thaumaturgos (or "the Wonderworker"). Origen exhorts Gregory to "extract from the philosophy of the Greeks what may serve as a course of study or a preparation for Christianity, and from geometry and astronomy what will serve to explain the sacred Scriptures" so that those intellectual resources can be put to use in furtherance of Christianity.[23] Origen elaborates on his point by referring to the events related in Exodus that we have just considered: "Perhaps something of this kind is shadowed forth in what is written in Exodus from the mouth of God, that the children of Israel were commanded to ask from their neighbors, and those who dwelt with them, vessels of silver and gold, and raiment, in order that, by spoiling the Egyptians, they might have material for the preparation of the things which pertained to the service of God."[24]

The chief point, as Origen explains to Gregory, is that "the Hebrews, guided by the wisdom of God, used for God's service" those things that had been improperly used by the Egyptians.[25] The treasures taken from the Egyptians were re-purposed for the greater glory of God, in much the same way that Origen urged Gregory to re-purpose his secular learning for the greater glory of God. For those of us looking back on Origen's writings with the knowledge that he would eventually be castigated for corrupting the Christian faith with Platonic philosophy, it is striking to note the warning that Origen goes on to make to Gregory: returning to Egypt, he says, is very dangerous. Those who "have subscribed to the law of God and the Israelite service of Him" ought not to "meddle with the knowledge of this world."[26] Origen gives another example to illustrate this further point.

[23]Origen, *Epistle to Gregory Thaumaturgus* § 1; trans. ANF vol. 4, p. 393.

[24]Ibid. § 2; trans. ANF 4, p. 393, slightly modified.

[25]Ibid. § 2; trans. ANF 4, p. 393.

[26]Ibid.

In contrast to the golden fittings of the sanctuary, Origen notes that golden calves were also made for the children of Israel to worship.[27] People who dwell in Egypt, Origen warns,

> are they who, from their Greek studies, produce heretical notions, and set them up, like the golden calf, in Bethel [1 Kg 12.29], which signifies "God's house." In these words also there seems to me an indication that they have set up their own imaginations in the Scriptures, where the word of God dwells, which is called in a figure Bethel.[28]

Origen is warning Gregory that the influence of Greek (i.e., pagan) learning has misguided some people into using the Egyptian spoils to make idols in the shape of their own thoughts, which they then worship instead of God. It is a sad irony that a theologian with such sensitivity to the hazards of careless recourse to philosophy would eventually be denounced on grounds that he was too reliant on philosophy in his writings.

Origen was not the only early theologian to contemplate the despoiling of the Egyptians in that way. Augustine of Hippo makes a brief but reasonably comprehensive statement of the metaphor in his *Confessions*, where he writes, "And I had come unto You from among the Gentiles, and I strained after that gold which You willed Your people to take from Egypt, seeing that wherever it was it was Yours."[29] Augustine's point is different from Origen's,

---

[27]Origen makes an error in this part of the letter, wrongly blaming Hadad the Edomite for having the idols made; his quotation of 1 Kg 12.28 makes it clear that he was actually thinking of King Jeroboam, who took up residence in Egypt after he had fled from King Solomon.

[28]Ibid., pp. 393–94.

[29]Augustine, *Confessions* 7.9.15.

whose letter had exhorted Gregory the Wonderworker to serve God. What Augustine stressed is that, because God is the source of everything good, all good things are properly God's.

On the basis of that theological insight, Augustine developed an account of Christian culture in which the Exodus plays a part. He wrote a treatise called *De doctrina christiana*, which is frequently translated with the nearest equivalent English words: *On Christian Doctrine*. But the Latin word *doctrina* does not share the limited connotations of the English word *doctrine*. *Doctrina* refers broadly to the process of teaching, training, and enculturation whereby one is introduced (even "indoctrinated") into a society, without any particular reference to religious belief. So what Augustine seeks to do in his book is to describe the ways in which Christian learning can be used to build up Christian society.

Like Origen's *Letter to Gregory Thaumaturgos*, Augustine's interest lies in the use of classical philosophy and philology—the spoils of the pagan heritage—to further a Christian exposition of the Scriptures. Secular learning is a mere trifle in comparison with what Augustine calls "the knowledge of the Holy Scripture."[30] Even more significant than its greater beauty is the fact that Holy Scripture acts as the criterion by which the value of secular learning can be determined:

> For whatever man may have learned from other sources, if it is hurtful, it is there condemned; if it is useful, it is therein contained. And while every man may find there all that he has learned of use elsewhere, he will find there in much greater abundance things that are to be found nowhere else,

[30]Augustine, *De doctrina christiana* 2.42.63, edited and translated by R. P. H. Green (Oxford: Clarendon Press, 1996).

but can be learned only in the wonderful sublimity and wonderful simplicity of the Scriptures.[31]

If that is the case, we might wonder what the value of secular learning is anyway. As Augustine indicates, basic instruction serves two purposes: first, it integrates the person being instructed into a larger group—that is, instruction has a social function; second, it enables that person to make sense of those "unknown signs" that might otherwise "be a hindrance" to understanding.[32] This learning is introductory. Deeper ambiguities, however, are not resolved by recourse to worldly learning, according to Augustine. In fact, those facets of the Scriptures are only to be approached by those who have become "meek and lowly of heart, subject to the easy yoke of Christ, and loaded with His light burden, rooted and grounded and built up in faith."[33] Humility is also implied in the student's willingness to learn from other people, and can be contrasted to the attitude of the proud of heart who reckon that they are worthy of being taught by God directly.[34]

The techniques that the diligent student needs are listed, and to some extent also explained, by Augustine. Chief among them is the understanding of foreign languages. For Augustine, this meant the ability to cope with basic biblical Hebrew and Greek in the first instance, but beyond that he expresses a preference for enough competence in those languages to be able to come to a critical opinion about translations.[35] We should pause here to take stock

[31]Ibid.

[32]Ibid.

[33]Ibid.

[34]See Augustine, *De doctrina christiana*, preface 7–18.

[35]Augustine, *De doctrina christiana* 2.34–35, 43.

of this point. Chiefly owing to his unflattering recollections of childhood exposure to Greek literature,[36] Augustine has garnered a reputation for linguistic incompetence. Comparison to Jerome, the "three-tongued man" who was famously learned in Latin, Greek, and Hebrew as Augustine himself acknowledged,[37] also does him no favors. The contrast with Jerome, however, reveals something noteworthy in Augustine's understanding of the canon of Scripture.

Unlike Jerome's argument that the canon should be limited to those books that were written in Hebrew,[38] Augustine's position was that the Christian canon of Scripture includes all the books that had been received as scriptural by those ancient and venerable churches that are the touchstones of orthodoxy.[39] Augustine echoed old claims that the Septuagint was itself the product of divine inspiration, even going so far as to say that, in cases of conflict, the Greek version be preferred to the witness of Hebrew texts.[40] In other words, even Scripture isn't simply an inert deposit

[36] Augustine, *Confessions* 14.23.

[37] Augustine, *City of God* 18.43.

[38] Jerome makes this clear in the "Preface to the Book of Kings" in his Vulgate translation. He evidently felt the need to defend his position, so he calls this his "armored preface . . . to all the books which we have translated from Hebrew to Latin, so that we may know that whatever is beyond them must take its place alongside the apocrypha."

[39] Augustine, *De doctrina christiana* 2.8; see also *City of God* 15.23, where Augustine comments on apocryphal legends that correspond to what we now know as the Book of Enoch.

[40] Augustine, *City of God* 18.36, 43; for a specific example of a conflict, see *City of God* 18.44. For an example of much older claims about the Septuagint, see Philo, *Life of Moses* 2.7.37.

from the past, as might be suggested by an archaeological definition of Scripture according to which it consists exclusively in
those books written in Hebrew and endorsed at a later date by
the rabbis. For Augustine, the Bible is identified explicitly as "the
Hebrew *and Christian* canonical Scriptures."[41] It is for that reason
that some understanding of Hebrew and Greek are appropriate
for Christian students of the Scriptures.

Such a student also needs to know about the "qualities of animals
or stones or plants or other things mentioned in the Scriptures
for the sake of some analogy."[42] Similarly, familiarity with math-
ematics, some understanding of music, and a grasp of the basic
principles of logic are prerequisite.[43] One requires a knowledge
of history, secular as well as sacred.[44]

Augustine finally acknowledges the value of certain arguments by
the philosophers, "especially the Platonists, which happen to be
true and consistent with our faith": these, he says, should

> be claimed for our own use, as it were from owners who
> have no right to them. Like the treasures of the ancient
> Egyptians, who possessed not only idols and heavy burdens
> which the people of Israel hated and shunned but also ves-
> sels and ornaments of silver and gold, and clothes, which on
> leaving Egypt the people of Israel, in order to make better use
> of them, surreptitiously claimed for themselves (they did this

[41]Augustine, *City of God* 15.23, emp. added.

[42]Augustine, *De doctrina christiana* 2.57 (I have slightly modified Green's
translation).

[43]Augustine, *De doctrina christiana* 2.62, 2.66, 2.117–28.

[44]Augustine, *De doctrina christiana* 2.105–8.

not on their own authority but at God's command, and the Egyptians in their ignorance actually gave them the things of which they had made poor use) . . . .[45]

Christians are likewise meant to "make better use" of the ornaments of pagan culture by putting it to the service of God.

* * *

At the climax of the second book of *De doctrina christiana*, before summarizing its key points, Augustine chose to refer to the Christian reaction to Platonism in terms of the Jewish despoiling of the Egyptians. By making it the crowning example in his analysis, Augustine calls additional attention to his typological reading of Exodus. So we need to pay attention to it and be prepared to find in it more than just a clever way of advocating basic skills like reading and writing. Remember what Augustine said in his *Confessions*: Christians have a claim to the good things of God wherever they are found, because those things are God's and Christians are of God's household. By no means are Christians uncritical or pre-critical in their recourse to these good things. It is not simply because they are the only things Christians know or are easily available in their surroundings that Christians recognize them as being good; rather, it is by reference to God who alone is good. They are tested and proven by God. This is one reason that Christianity is not contaminated through contact with foreign ideas and practices.

Augustine believed that, in comparison to the glories of Jerusalem, the riches taken out of Egypt were but tinsel. But that comparison does not mean that Christians are excused from engaging with

[45]Augustine, *De doctrina christiana* 2.144.

society at large. It does not justify sectarian complacency. The point of invoking the despoiling of the Egyptians is precisely that Christians should be prepared to find worthwhile and valuable information from sources outside of the Christian community.

If we step back now to think about what we have seen from both Augustine and Origen, we can appreciate how that episode in the exodus from Egypt gave early Christians an opportunity to express the serious interest they themselves took in the cultural heritage that was theirs as *Gentile* Christians. This is evidence that they were shrewdly aware that there are important things to appropriate from outside the community of believers. Prompted by reflection on God's command to the Jews to abscond with Egyptian gold, silver, and finery, the early Christians worked out a theory that would justify incorporating foreign elements into their theology without fear of contamination. The *De doctina christiana* is an educational syllabus that justifies building up a Christian culture. It can be regarded as an invitation for Christians to engage constructively with secular society. Augustine's invitation has been taken up, time and again, with the result that *De doctrina christiana* has become a fundamental document in the history of western Christian culture.

To take up that task by imitating this serious interest in constructive engagement means that we can look to patristics for a vantage from which to criticize our society. Criticism here does not refer to mean-spirited sniping or smug faultfinding, but to acting with discernment. The lesson taken from Exodus 3.22 and related verses as mediated through Origen and Augustine means that we should expect to find intimations of God's handiwork everywhere and that we ought not to be embarrassed by acknowledging God's truth where we find it. Being Christian—even, let it be noted, being Christian in a deliberately patristic way—is not a matter of simply opting out from society. Instead, following their example we employ godly criteria to assess and evaluate society. Through imitating the Fathers in this way, the patristic legacy becomes the basis for engaging critically with the modern world.

To engage with the modern world in this way is not to betray or abandon the past. It is rather to negotiate through the present with the benefit of experience. For that to be possible, we have to get beyond a narrow obsession with the past (which would induce paralysis) at the same time that we use what we have learned to evaluate the circumstances in which we find ourselves. We are then able to make informed decisions about what to identify with and make our own in those circumstances. This is obviously an entirely different thing from archiving records of the past to ensure that no scraps are lost owing to the passage of time or the selectivity of collective attention. Rather, it is a responsible use of evidence from the past that can serve as the basis for principled action in the present. George Santayana offers a useful elucidation of this principle:

> Progress, far from consisting in change, depends on reten-tiveness. When change is absolute there remains no being to improve and no direction is set for possible improvement: and when experience is not retained, as among savages, infancy is perpetual. Those who cannot remember the past are condemned to repeat it. In the first stage of life the mind is frivolous and easily distracted; it misses progress by fail-ing in consecutiveness and persistence. This is the condition of children and barbarians, in whom instinct has learned

nothing from experience. In a second stage men are docile to events, plastic to new habits and suggestions, yet able to graft them on original instincts, which they thus bring to fuller satisfaction. This is the plane of manhood and true progress.[46]

## Beyond doctrine

If we want to join the early fathers in "despoiling the Egyptians" and imitate them in making the best of the world in which we find ourselves as Christians, we will find fairly quickly that there is more to living patristically than carefully articulating theological doctrines to rejoice the angels and refute the heretics. According to a helpful definition from Christian antiquity, "Christianity is Christ our Savior's teaching, which consists of ascetical struggling, understanding nature, and conversing with God."[47] Those undertakings—striving to live ethically through ascetic practices, to understand the physical and material order as the handiwork of God, and to live with and speak to and of God—are all areas in which it is possible for us to learn from ancient Christianity. The ancient church has given us guidance, not just slogans. So in this final section, we will look at examples from the patristic legacy that are relevant to Orthodox living in the modern world.

The first example is a word that, in modern terms, refers to an important aspect of social justice: *philoptôcheia*, or "care for the poor." As we will see from the examples of Basil the Great and

[46]George Santayana, *The Life of Reason: Or the Phases of Human Progress*, vol. 1 (London: Constable, 1906), pp. 284–85.

[47]Evagrius Ponticus, *Praktikos* 1 (an admittedly free translation of the last three terms: πρακτικῆς καὶ φυσικῆς καὶ θεολογικῆς).

John Chrysostom, we are exhorted to enact our beliefs by behaving in a considered way to benefit those who are unable to help themselves. The second instance that we will take up is less social and more private. It is the application of ancient monastic advice about constancy, or stability, to a modern condition that is widespread but often difficult to diagnose. Here, the central word in Greek is *akêdia*.

## St Basil the Great

In addition to being a remarkable theologian, churchman, and author, Basil the Great (c.330–January 1, 379) was renowned during his own lifetime for his tremendous efforts to provide shelter, food, and even medical attention for the poor of his area. Sozomen, a historian of the church who wrote in the 440's, drew particular attention to the foundation that Basil established to that end: "the Basileias, the most celebrated hospice for the poor [ . . . ] was established by Basil, bishop of Caesarea, from whom it received its name in the beginning, and retains it until to-day."[48] That Basil should have demonstrated such concern for the well being of the destitute was no surprise to his long-time friend and colleague, Gregory of Nazianzus. Gregory describes Basil's family background in these terms:

> The union of his parents, cemented as it was by a community
> of virtue, no less than by cohabitation, was notable for many
> reasons, especially for generosity to the poor, for hospitality,
> for purity of soul as the result of self-discipline, for the dedi-
> cation to God of a portion of their property (a matter not as

---

[48]Sozomen, *Ecclesiastical History* 6.34.9; trans. NPNF, second series, vol. 2, p. 371.

yet so much cared for by most men, as it now has grown to be, in consequence of such previous examples as have given distinction to it), and for all those other points, which have been published throughout Pontus and Cappadocia, to the satisfaction of many . . . .[49]

All these fine charitable accomplishments notwithstanding, however, Gregory's view was that Basil's parents' most distinguished accomplishment was in rearing their children who had emerged as outstanding Christian leaders.

Basil himself was evidently inspired by his parents' example of civic service, but was more thoroughgoing in pursuing it. (This was possible for him in part because he lived a life of monastic celibacy.) Gregory tells us that as a young man Basil found it necessary to study medicine because of "his physical delicacy, and his care of the sick."[50] The last clause may reflect Gregory's benefit of hindsight: a basic grasp of medical principles was within the range of what Basil might have taken an interest in as the beneficiary of a liberal education, without having any particular aspiration to practice medicine. In any case, as Sozomen relates, Basil established a hospice that provided food, shelter, and care for the destitute and for lepers. Gregory likened this establishment to a city nobler than several ancient cities and foundations, naming in particular Thebes, Babylon, the Colossus of Rhodes, the Great Pyramid, and the Mausoleum at Halicarnassus. His description is expansive:

[49]Gregory of Nazianzus, *Oration* 43.9; trans. NPNF, second series, vol. 7, p. 594, slightly modified.

[50]Gregory of Nazianzus, *Oration* 43.23 (p. 601).

> Go forth a little way from the city, and behold the new city,
> the storehouse of piety, the common treasury of the wealthy,
> in which the superfluities of their wealth, yes, and even their
> necessaries, are stored, in consequence of his exhortations,
> freed from the power of the moth [cf. Mt 6.19], no longer
> gladdening the eyes of the thief, and escaping both the emu-
> lation of envy, and the corruption of time: where disease is
> regarded in a religious light, and disaster is thought a bless-
> ing, and sympathy is put to the test.[51]

Despite this grand description, we have no way of knowing precisely how large the establishment was. But ultimately the size
of the operation was less important than the fact that it put into
action Basil's awareness that the indigent and diseased poor are
nevertheless part of the Body of Christ.

Basil taught others by his example. He "took the lead in pressing
upon those who were men, that they ought not to despise their
fellowmen, nor to dishonor Christ, the one Head of all, by their
inhuman treatment of them; but to use the misfortunes of others
as an opportunity of firmly establishing their own lot, and to lend
to God that mercy of which they stand in need at His hands."[52]
The reference to lending to God in that passage is shocking. In
what sense can a human creature possibly *lend* anything to God
the Creator? Even more surprisingly, how can a human lend God
*mercy*? This is a bold claim, no doubt, but it can be seen as an
extension of a well-established principle of Biblical ethics: God

---

[51]Gregory of Nazianzus, *Oration* 43.62 (pp. 618–9).

[52]Ibid. By citing this oration in an old translation, I have taken up its gender
biases intact. It seems to me that Gregory's point could be conveyed by a
play on the words "human" and "humane."

has a special care for the poor, such that our deeds toward the poor are actually deeds toward God.

For instance, we read in Proverbs 14.31 (LXX), "Those who oppress the poor provoke their own Maker, but they who honor Him show mercy upon the beggar." The Lord makes the same basic point, in his parable about the separation of the sheep and the goats (Mt 25.34–40):

> Then the King will say to those on his right, "Come, you who are blessed by my Father; take your inheritance, the kingdom prepared for you since the creation of the world. For I was hungry and you gave me something to eat, I was thirsty and you gave me something to drink, I was a stranger and you invited me in, I needed clothes and you clothed me, I was sick and you looked after me, I was in prison and you came to visit me."

> Then the righteous will answer him, "Lord, when did we see you hungry and feed you, or thirsty and give you something to drink? When did we see you a stranger and invite you in, or needing clothes and clothe you? When did we see you sick or in prison and go to visit you?"

> The King will reply, "I tell you the truth, whatever you did for one of the least of these brothers of mine, you did for me."

By showing mercy to God in the persons of the poor, we can look forward to reciprocal mercy from God. Through acts of charity, we can build up a relationship with God that Gregory of Nazianzus can audaciously describe as "lending mercy to God."

In these examples, we have been looking at the way Gregory described the life of Basil. There is a slight remove here: it is not how Basil described his own care for the poor, but how Basil's friend described it. However, we can find a direct statement of the patristic ideal of care for the poor from the most celebrated preacher in the history of the Greek Church, Basil's near contemporary, John Chrysostom.

## St John Chrysostom

Chrysostom was from Antioch, where he gained a reputation for being a truly outstanding preacher. While a young man in Syria, Chrysostom gained firsthand experience of ascetical living with the monks who lived in the mountains. Chrysostom left Antioch in 398, when he became bishop of Constantinople. His tenure in the see of Constantinople was relatively brief and stormy, in part because he brought his monastic sensibility to his preaching in a way that alienated and offended powerful people in society, notably Empress Eudoxia. Twice Chrysostom was expelled from Constantinople, and during his second exile he died. One theme in the message that Chrysostom paid such a great personal cost to proclaim was Christian charity.

It was (and often still is) difficult to stir the Christian community to activity, to bring the beauty of Christianity outside of the buildings in which Christians worship. Chrysostom urged the faithful to take action by using a very striking image: he likened care for the poor to service within the temple. The altar is naturally the focal point for our attention: "Would you see His altar also? Bezaleel built it not [see Ex 31.1–11], nor any other but God Himself; not of stones, but of a material brighter than the heaven, of reasonable souls."[53] The all-important difference between worship in the Temple and Christian care for the poor is the next point made by Chrysostom: "But the priest enters into the holy of holies. Into yet more awful places you may enter when you offer this sacrifice, where none is present but 'thy Father, Which seeth in secret,' (Mt 6.4.) where no other beholds."

Chrysostom then anticipates the obvious problem: in what sense can it possibly be the case that charity exercised in the marketplace can be compared to the High Priest withdrawing from the public into the Holy of Holies? His answer is that Christ instructs us specifically not to give alms *so as to be seen* by others (see Mt 6.1). So what matters is less whether we are seen than what motivates our actions. When we make an offering to the poor, says Chrysostom, we are putting a sacrifice upon the very "body of the Lord."

Chrysostom even claims boldly that the sacrifice of giving to the poor is preferable to worship at the eucharistic altar, because the poor actually make present Christ himself, and Christ's presence conveys special honor upon the gift. The altar within the church "is but a stone by nature, but becomes holy because it receives Christ's Body," whereas the altar of the poor "is holy because it is itself Christ's Body." With this comparison in mind, Chrysostom is able to appeal to a sense of respect that his audience have for the furnishings of the Church. And this in turn enables him to point out that it is as perverse to neglect the poor as it would be to allow the Church's altar to fall into a state of disrepair. By contrast, the giving of alms is itself an act of prayer, as Chrysostom indicates

[53] John Chrysostom, *On Second Corinthians, Homily* 20:3; trans. NPNF, first series, vol. 12, p. 374. Until further noted, the following quotations are from the same homily and have been modified slightly.

with a quotation from Acts 10.4: the gift given "passes beyond the heaven itself, and the heaven of heaven, and arrives even at the throne of the King. For, 'Thy prayers,' he says, 'and thine alms are come up before God.'"

Chrysostom frequently repeated his concern for the well being of the destitute. In another homily, after berating his listeners for regarding the poor as being less worthy than their slaves and even less worthy than their dogs, he emphasizes the privilege that the poor will have on that great and terrible day: "For he will stand by you in the Day of Judgment, and will deliver you from the fire. What do all your slaves do like this? When Tabitha died, who raised her up? The slaves who stood around or the poor?"[54] Tabitha, as the faithful well knew, "was always doing good and helping the poor"(Acts 9.36), and it was the widows who were noted in particular as wailing at her bier and showing Peter the clothes that she had made and given to the poor (Acts 9.39).

In another homily, Chrysostom dwelt on the role of the poor as God's proxies. Reflecting on the parable of the sheep and the goats, Chrysostom went beyond the remarks that we considered earlier, which seemed to suggest a disregard for the formal worship of the community and the priestly order who minister it. What we read in this homily points instead to the convergence of a concern for furnishing the Church's worship and a regard for the needy, in that both are ways of showing one's devotion to Christ:

> For what is the profit, when His table indeed is full of golden cups, but He perishes with hunger? First fill Him, being hungry, and then abundantly deck out His table also. Do you

---

[54]John Chrysostom, *Homilies on the Epistle to the Hebrews* 11.7; trans. NPNF, first series, vol. 14, pp. 420–21.

---

make Him a cup of gold, while not giving Him a cup of cold water? And what is the profit? Do you furnish His table with cloths bespangled with gold, while affording to Himself not even the necessary covering? And what good comes of it? For tell me, should you see one at a loss for necessary food, and omit appeasing his hunger, while you first overlaid his table with silver; would he indeed thank you, and not rather be indignant? What, again, if seeing one wrapped in rags, and stiff with cold, you should neglect giving him a garment, and build golden columns, saying, "you were doing it to his honor," would he not say that you were mocking, and account it an insult, and that the most extreme?[55]

Even though Chrysostom himself never seems to have used the phrase, all the same it is reasonable for modern interpreters to talk about this aspect of his preaching as a way of advocating the "liturgy after the liturgy."

In current usage the word *liturgy* refers to the organized worship of the Church in general and to the Eucharistic Liturgy in particular. But in earlier times, the word λειτουργία referred not just to acts of religious worship but also to the civic duty that one has toward the poor. That civic duty is not merely a secular responsibility: it is also an expression of religious sentiment, since in the classical world the public order was understood in terms of a cosmic (and therefore a *sacred*) order. So when Chrysostom made a robust connection between eucharistic worship and civic care for the poor, he was not doing anything unprecedented. True, his description of social engagement as fundamentally realizing the same impulse as the eucharistic liturgy is theologically articu-

[55]John Chrysostom, *Homilies on Matthew* 50.4; trans. NPNF, first series, vol. 10, p. 303, modified.

late to an uncommon degree. Chrysostom's clarity results from bringing back into focus the long-established social relevance of the term *leitourgia*. Through his homilies, he underlined the fact that the social responsibility to feed, clothe, and shelter the poor, on the one hand, and the acts of religious devotion that can (but need not) be considered formal worship, on the other, are mutually complementary.

Both of those senses of the word are well attested in Graeco-Roman sources, in Jewish sources (both rabbinic and Hellenistic, the most striking example of the latter being in the Book of Tobit, found in the Septuagint), and in Christian scriptures and later writings.[56] For example, the word is frequently used in the epistles of St Paul to designate both the service of making voluntary collections for the poor and the service of giving thanks to God (see 2 Cor 9.12, Philem 2.7, and Rom 15.27). We find in the *Shepherd of Hermas* (written in the second century) that the word can refer to Christian service in a general way: "Only continue humble, and serve (*leitourgôn*) the Lord in all purity of heart, you and your children, and your house, and walk in my commands which I enjoin upon you, and your repentance will be deep and pure; and if you observe these things with your household, every affliction will depart from you. And affliction, he added, will depart from all who walk in these my commandments."[57] Gradually, this general

[56]See the first chapter of Susan R. Holman, *The Hungry Are Dying: Beggars and Bishops in Roman Cappadocia*, Oxford Studies in Historical Theology (New York: Oxford University Press, 2001), pp. 31–63: "Leitourgia and the Poor in the Early Christian World"; and, for the general social setting, Peter Brown, *Poverty and Leadership in the Later Roman Empire* (Hanover and London: University Press of New England, 2002).

[57]*Shepherd of Hermas*, Similitude 7.6; trans. ANF vol. 2, p. 39.

sense of the term was eclipsed by its usage to designate organized rituals of worship. So what Chrysostom was doing with his homilies was recalling to the mind of the faithful their religious duties and giving those duties a renewed urgency by reverting to the standard ancient term for it (*leitourgia*), in full knowledge that the term now bore additional associations with the formal patterns of prayer and worship within the church building.

From Chrysostom's reassertion of the earlier, dual meaning of the term *leitourgia*, we can see that patristic evidence itself cautions us against thinking of liturgical worship (even the Divine Liturgy itself) exclusively as an event for insiders. These days the idea is widespread that the liturgy is a mysterious, solemn form of worship that is foreign to our workaday life. It may be that this idea is deeply comforting: it makes of the liturgy an oasis in the wasteland of secular life. But at the same time, thinking of the liturgy primarily as an event within and for the benefit of the assembled faithful cannot allow us to forget that liturgy is *also* a movement whereby the faithful reach out from worshipping God within the community toward those who are not necessarily party to that worship, so that they can have a share in the benefits (social, material, even spiritual) that accrue to the liturgical assembly.

We noted that John Chrysostom's early formation was in the company of monks living in the Syrian mountains. This experience informed Chrysostom's outlook on Christian living, as is evident from the tone of the exhortations to the assembled faithful that we have been taking into account.[58] Chrysostom encourages an ascetical detachment from possessions, which frees secular Christians

---

[58]Also worth attention in this context is the homily ("Baptismal Homily 8") that Chrysostom preached when a group of monks visited Antioch.

so that they can give liberally to the poor and disenfranchised. The other interesting feature in Chrysostom's homilies is the surprising, almost anti-clerical overtone that we find in them. This is seen in Chrysostom's suggestions that, by donating to the poor, lay Christians can make a sacrifice that surpasses the eucharistic sacrifice offered by the clergy. We have already looked into how Chrysostom identified the similarity in both activities precisely as forms of *liturgy*. More could be said about the respective roles of the clergy and the laity, on the basis of Chrysostom's preaching, but let us now turn to another example from the patristic tradition, a monastic insight that is applicable to life in the modern world.

## Monks and Nuns

To provide some context, we will begin with a look at some of the ways in which monastic living has impacted upon secular Christian life within the patristic tradition. Although the archetypal monk is the hermit, monasticism was firmly imbedded in cities from an early stage. Even the "Father of Monasticism," Anthony the Great (c. 251–356), was able to find monastic tutors in the near vicinity of the villages:

> Now there was then in the next village an old man who had lived the life of a hermit from his youth up. Anthony, after he had seen this man, imitated him in piety. And at first he began to abide in places outside the village: then if he heard of a good man anywhere, like the prudent bee, he went forth and sought him, nor turned back to his own palace until he had seen him; and he returned, having got from the good man as it were supplies for his journey in the way of virtue. So dwelling there at first, he confirmed his purpose not to

return to the abode of his fathers nor to the remembrance of his kinsfolk; but to keep all his desire and energy for perfecting his discipline.[59]

Even Anthony was not cut off from society; in this, he was followed by other hermits who were available to those "in the world" for guidance, healing, and instruction.[60]

Within a generation of the deaths of Anthony, who pioneered eremitic life, and Pachomius (c. 292–348), who organized several Egyptian monasteries into a confederation of coenobitic monks and nuns, monasteries were beginning to appear in major cities. A petition lodged in 448 indicates that at least 23 monasteries were established in or around Constantinople over the course of about 50 years from ca. 380.[61] In the course of the fifth century, two extremely important monasteries were established: the Monastery of the Akoimetoi (c. 440) and the Studite Monastery (462). The presence of so many monasteries within the Queen

[59] Athanasius, *The Life of Anthony* 3; trans. NPNF, second series, vol. 4, p. 196, modified slightly.

[60] The seminal modern study on this topic is Peter Brown's "The Rise and Function of the Holy Man in Late Antiquity," *The Journal of Roman Studies* 61 (1971): 80–101, reprinted with modifications in his *Society and the Holy in Late Antiquity* (Berkeley: University of California Press, 1982): 103–52. The twenty-fifth anniversary of this publication was marked by a conference in the University of California, Berkeley, reviewing and extending the central thesis; the conference in turn led to a special issue of the *Journal of Early Christian Studies* for the Fall of 1998 (issue 6.4), edited by Susanna Elm and Naomi Janowitz. For a sound assessment of those essays in relation to Brown's original work, see now John Howe, "Revisiting the Holy Man," *The Catholic Historical Review* 86 (2000): 640–44.

[61] See Peter Hatlie, *The Monks and Monasteries of Constantinople* ca. 350–850 (Cambridge, UK: Cambridge University Press, 2007), Appendix 1.

City ensured that monks and nuns would be visible within society and would enable them to take an active part in social life.[62]

Earlier, when we were thinking about John Chrysostom's tenure in Constantinople, it emerged that Chrysostom's ascetic preaching profoundly irritated people like the empress. Being a social gadfly is certainly one role that monks can play in society. But it isn't their only role. Evidence indicates that monks were *not* uniformly unpopular within society. They were able to make favorable impressions even in highest social echelons. For instance, one of our most valuable sources on Egyptian monasticism during its glory days in the last decades of the fourth century was written by Palladius of Helenopolis for the edification of the imperial chamberlain, Lausus, on account of which it is known as the *Lausiac History*. Still later, the high regard that Emperor Justinian I (482/3–565; emperor from 527) had for monks was reflected in the legal reforms that he pursued: among other things, Justinian provided legal protection for monks in civic contexts.[63] The involvement of nuns and monks in Constantinopolitan life and society was complex, of course, but they continued to be involved in the life of the city for many centuries.

Not only could the monks go from the monasteries into the courts and marketplaces, secular Christians could of course go to the monasteries. A good example is provided in the descriptions of the Convent of Trikhinareas. Established by Eleftheria, a *koubikoularia* or lady-in-waiting to Empress Pulcheria, for herself and her friends, the convent housed about 70 women who were from such

[62]Hatlie's *Monks and Monasteries of Constantinople* is an important, extended analysis of the many roles played in Constantinopolitan life by the monks and nuns.

[63]See Hatlie, *Monks and Monasteries of Constantinople*, pp. 50–51.

well-to-do families that they actually financed the establishment themselves.[64] This indicates that monastic teaching could be well received by members of high society. The convent was a conspicuous center for the Orthodox resistance to the iconoclastic policies of Emperor Constantine V (718–775; emperor from 741).[65]

Monasticism continued to influence the life of the Church in subsequent centuries.[66] In modern times and especially since the eighteenth century, monasticism has become a conspicuous and important part of Orthodox Christianity. Significantly, this upsurge of monasticism has been accompanied by a renewed circulation of early Christian ascetical literature amongst secular Christians. Through this resurgence, the techniques for cultivating a Christian spirit that were painstakingly developed by monks over centuries are achieving what is in all likelihood a wider circulation than ever before. As a specimen, let us take the example of *akêdia*.[67]

The term is almost impossible to translate satisfactorily, because it describes a condition of familiar elements that, despite their

[64]See *Life of Auxentius* 61 (text in Migne's *Patrologia Graeca*, vol. 114, column 1429C); and further M.-F. Auxepy, "Les *Vies d'Auxence* et le monachisme 'auxentien'," *Revue des Etudes Byzantines* 53 (1995): 205–35.

[65]See *Life of Stephen the Younger* 13 and 34 (ed. and trans. M.-F. Auxepy, *La Vie d'Étienne le Jeune par Étienne le Diacre*, Birmingham Byzantine and Ottoman Monographs 3 (Aldershot: Ashgate, 1997), pp. 104–5 and 133–34 (texts), 198 and 228–29 (translations).

[66]See Rosemary Morris, *Monks and Laymen in Byzantium, 843–1118* (Cambridge, UK: Cambridge University Press, 1995).

[67]The best book on *akêdia* is Gabriel Bunge's *Akèdia. La doctrine spirituelle d'Évagre le Pontique sur l'acédie* (Bégrolles-en-Mauges: Abbaye de Bellefontaine, 1991). Available in English translation as *Despondency: The Spiritual Teaching of Evagrius of Pontus* (Crestwood, NY: St Vladimir's Seminary Press, 2012).

familiarity, is not universal in this particular configuration. Some rough approximations include listlessness, ennui, and despair. Better than supplying a word that has its own potentially irrelevant, or even misleading connotations, we can refer to a firsthand account of the experience from a Desert Father. Describing *akêdia* as an attacking force that besets the monk, especially the solitary monk, John Cassian writes:

> [He] looks about anxiously this way and that, and sighs that none of the brethren come to see him, and often goes in and out of his cell, and frequently gazes up at the sun, as if it was too slow in setting, and so a kind of unreasonable confusion of mind takes possession of him like some foul darkness, and makes him idle and useless for every spiritual work, so that he imagines that no cure for so terrible an attack can be found in anything except visiting some one of the brethren, or in the solace of sleep alone. Then the disease suggests that he ought to show courteous and friendly hospitalities to the brethren, and pay visits to the sick, whether near at hand or far off. He talks too about some dutiful and religious offices; that those kinsfolk ought to be inquired after, and that he ought to go and see them oftener; that it would be a real work of piety to go more frequently to visit that religious woman, devoted to the service of God, who is deprived of all support of kindred; and that it would be a most excellent thing to get what is needful for her who is neglected and despised by her own kinsfolk; and that he ought piously to devote his time to these things instead of staying uselessly and with no profit in his cell.[68]

[68]John Cassian, *Institutes* 10.2; trans. NPNF, second series, vol. 11, p. 267.

The symptoms of this spiritual disease are of course keyed in to the monastic life in Cassian's account, but it is easy to identify with it by making a few changes—by substituting e-mails and coffee breaks for gazing at the sun and going in and out of one's cell. What makes the account vivid is not only Cassian's brilliant insight into the workings of the soul, but also the fact that being able to recognize a fidgety spirit and the damage it can do is a part of Orthodox life that we can recognize immediately.

*　*　*

Secular life is full of beguiling distractions. It is understandable that people who are trying to lead a life of purpose will regard these distractions as a problem. Yet it is not always easy to find a way to articulate that feeling. The literature of patristic monasticism provides a set of criteria for making sense of these distractions and a vocabulary for explaining why they are problematic. In a society consumed by entertainment and leisure, Cassian's diagnosis of *akêdia* cuts through proliferating and vacuous nonsense.

It may help to give a sense for how unusual it is to regard distractions so seriously by bringing in another example of religious counsel from a surprising source, which discourages the following activities (among others):

> Daily socialising [*sic*] with the intention to have fun and kill time. Sleeping a lot and chilling out. Chatting on the phone for hours. Ignoring duties/responsibilities and prefer [*sic*] to rest, slack and be lazy. Exceeding one's involvement in sport activities. Diverting from the serious, fruitful work to wasting time. Playing on the internet with no need. Looking for

excuses not to do any duties as he is bored with doing them. Window shopping and spending hours in the market. Going to cinemas and restaurants to eat out.

Most of this advice is consistent with a modern diagnosis of *akêdia*. So it may come as a surprise to learn that the list is taken from a publication on boredom from al-Muhajiroun, a militant Islamic movement.[69]

Both accounts identify problematic aspects of modern life and redress them by calling for discipline and seriousness of a distinctly religious type. The similar diagnosis shouldn't be taken to suggest that Christian monasticism is (or should be) extremist in political, much less militant, terms. There are major differences between the position advocated by al-Muhajiroun and Cassian's strategy for overcoming *akêdia*. For instance, the former advocates escape, in order to create a social separation between its adherents and the rest of society, whereas the latter advocates entering more deeply into the circumstances that are eliciting *akêdia*.

Without disparaging society, Cassian encourages a re-doubling of efforts to pray and especially to undertake manual labor.[70] Cassian's advice is applicable by secular Christians with very little modification, as will be recognized by those who have learned to introduce prayer into repetitive activities such as gardening, baking bread, washing dishes, even mowing the lawn. Beyond this, we see that Cassian's advice amounts to a call to enter more deeply into the particularities of our daily life in a prayerful way,

---

[69]See Quintan Wiktorowicz, *Radical Islam Rising: Muslim Extremism in the West* (Lanham, MD: Rowman and Littlefield, 2005), pp. 57–58.

[70]See Cassian, *Institutes* 10.10–14.

rather than to succumb to the temptation to flee from them in a misbegotten desire to find satisfaction elsewhere. Cassian's advice is in line with counsel from the Scriptures: "Whatever your hand finds to do, do it with all your might" (Eccl 9.10 LXX).

Identifying *akêdia* as a symptom of spiritual sickness is an example of taking up the legacy of ancient Christian monasticism. When we accept that *akêdia* is a real crisis, we are able to ascertain a problem in situations where previously we might only have been vaguely aware that somewhere something was somehow going wrong. At the same time, this use of the patristic heritage of monasticism gives us a powerful tool for a critique of culture. It tells against thinking that boredom is a nuisance to be relieved (often, through spending money), and instead motivates us to look for a deeper problem. Instead of killing time, we begin to look for ways to redeem the time.

In other words, in secular life we learn to apply the lessons that are available to us from the patristic heritage of monasticism; even those of us who are not living monastically can learn to live more ascetically. The case of *akêdia* highlights a double transformation within the patristic tradition. In the first place, an idea is retrieved from the ancient world for use today. The relevance of the idea is not necessarily self-evident, because it maps out a psychological experience that may be slightly familiar but is basically foreign to our society. Its retrieval is a complex process of intuitively recognizing something that might be serviceable, and then making it useful. That level of transformation is in principle common whenever we look back and take up something from antiquity, whether or not we are thinking specifically about Christian antiquity.

In the second place, the idea is a particular component of monastic culture. When it is used as a diagnostic tool for secular Christians in a digital, consumer world, it has to be re-interpreted for use outside of monasteries. What is required is not an automatic transference of practices honed for monks and nuns and an immediate implementation of them by schoolteachers and accountants. It goes deeper than simply urging a family to assimilate as closely as possible to a monastic community. Instead, we need to engage with this monastic concept in a patient and creative way, so that a doubly foreign idea can be made to support Christian life "in the world."

# WHAT'S NEXT?

Since the publication of Paul Valliere's *Modern Russian Theology*, many commentators have hailed the resurgent interest in the theology of Fr Sergius Bulgakov and in other specimens of Russian religious philosophy from the early twentieth century. Increased scope for studying Orthodox theology is welcome. But the tone of some commentaries oddly suggests that contemporary Orthodox theological research is a zero-sum game, implying that renewed theological enthusiasm for recent Russian theologians, by its very existence, diminishes the theological value of the modern study of patristic theology. Not all commentators' rhetoric is so lacking in nuance, of course. Students of Bulgakov's work have established beyond any doubt that patristic theology influenced his thinking, much as it influenced other kindred modern Orthodox theologians. The sharp dichotomy between Russian religious philosophy and the neo-patristic synthesis is more apparent than real, better fit to generate ephemeral academic pieces than to illuminate recent historic episodes. The question is not *whether* modern Orthodox theology should be influenced by Christian antiquity, but *how* it should be influenced. A host of further questions about how patristic theology is appropriated in the modern world remain. It seems good in these final pages to say something about the relevance of patristic studies—something that is questioned by several commentators today.

Valliere, for example, rejects the neo-patristic synthesis, alleging that patristic sources are not sufficiently relevant to modern life. He seems to be suggesting that, to be relevant, patristic material has to speak directly to the modern reader. If we reject this suggestion, as I believe we should, we need to be cautious about another pitfall. Some of Zizioulas's detractors criticize him for attributing distinctly modern concerns to the ancients, for reading contemporary philosophical trends directly into ancient texts. However flawed these criticisms are, they rightly call for clarity and honesty when we moderns make claims about what we find when we read earlier texts. Though we may disagree with Valliere and with Zizioulas's critics, the best way to address their concerns would be to read widely and deeply within the patristic heritage and to assume responsibility for the use that we make now of that heritage.

A major prop to their critique (which has not to my knowledge received adequate attention) is the presumption that all Orthodox theologians must work in unison. Consensus is privileged for its own sake, and made a rule. The prominence given in some quarters to sophiology—a doctrine that allegedly makes a signature contribution to Orthodox theology (perhaps even a distinct Orthodox contribution to Christian theology as a whole, since many enthusiastic advocates are not Orthodox)—makes sense in this context. It is a shibboleth. To be a really *modern* Orthodox theologian is ostensibly to embroil oneself within internecine debates that racked the Russian immigrant community in Paris during the first half of the last century. Attempts supplanting neo-patristic theology, seen in that light, are a bid for dominance not simply for a group of likeminded scholars, but more significantly also for a specific moment in the recent history of Orthodox Christianity.

Now there is danger of being swept away by the notion that all Orthodox theology must move like a juggernaut. To the contrary, what we have seen in the course of this book gives us reasons to think that Orthodox theology has typically not been monolithic. The perpetuation across history of witness to the renewal of life in Christ is a complex and untidy process. Textbooks that present a linear, thematic progression of Orthodox doctrine are suitable for an initial approach to the subject and can be appreciated as such, but should in due course be put away with the other "childish things" of which St Paul wrote. Moving beyond highly schematized (and often highly romanticized) views of the past is aided by recourse to the skills, techniques, and attitudes that patristic theology at its best promotes.

To say that is what patristic theology promotes *at its best* is as much as to acknowledge that we often fall short of that level. A fault characteristic of modern Orthodox patristics is the same timorous preoccupation with consensus that, I have suggested, props up claims that the neo-patristic synthesis is being supplanted by Russian religious philosophy. For different reasons, the image of Orthodox theology as a juggernaut is equally problematic in both cases. The problem within the neo-patristic synthesis is that presuming Orthodoxy is monolithic leads to (or perhaps legitimates) *collectivism*—something that entails a wide array of problems: prescriptive frames of reference for interpretation, closed canons of sources suitable for study, concentrated allocation of resources (intellectual, financial, and institutional) in furtherance of narrow interests, promotion of the artificial consensus thus generated, and a general withering of creative and productive research. These major problems limit the scope and the method of contemporary Orthodox patristic study. Presuming homogeneity within Orthodox patristic study leads to reduced circumstances in which the ability to manipulate symbolic terms is prized more than the ability to explicate the meaning of those terms (something we considered in Chapter 3, above), in which ancient canons are used more often to *exclude* new things than to *measure* them. It stultifies serious, disciplined, and creative engagement with historical sources.

In the first chapter of this book, I referred to a range of topics connected to the term *patristic*. There, I alluded to the assimilation of patristic theology to early Christian studies. The challenges that emerge when evidence of particular theological significance begin to be valued by scholars with non-theological (sometimes anti-theological) interests in that evidence are myriad. Adequately responding to those challenges requires sustained, careful, systematic reflection on the theological value of the evidence and painstaking exposition of its theological value for modern Christians. By contrast, it is inadequate to respond to the challenges by asserting a prior claim upon the evidence ("These texts are *ours*; they are only available to you to study because our forebears preserved them!"). It is also inadequate to respond by extending theological banalities beyond their familiar application to classic theological texts, so as to keep up with (for instance) scholarly enthusiasm for erstwhile heresies ("X and Y really didn't disagree about anything of substance after all; that is merely how it seems to less sophisticated readers").

---

Perhaps the worst use that can be made of patristic studies is the attempt to hotwire it into other sophisticated conversations. I trust it is superfluous by this point to say that I do not believe in isolationism. Even so, there is something stunningly presumptuous about how casually theologians from time to time will issue a call for "integration" between patristic theology and (let's say) modern science, public policy, or aesthetics. What is presumptuous is the radical reduction of patristic theology to a single known quantity that can be manipulated into a mutually advantageous relationship with some other domain of humane learning (often itself similarly reduced). On the few occasions I myself have witnessed such bold cries, they all have resulted in nothing more substantial than a position paper that might boast glimmers of insight but more frequently vanishes without a trace. The problem comes not from sheer incommensurability between patristics and whatever "conversation partner" has been designated for it, but rather from the idiosyncrasies that proliferate when the theologian in question attempts to render down centuries of theology into manageable proportions. These idiosyncrasies typically result from deploying common sense about modern Orthodoxy as the standard to identify what is pertinent, across the narrow range of themes and theologians who are readily available in modern translations. Theologians undertaking that task tend to make embarrassing mistakes from the very moment that they set foot outside their field of expertise.

What, then, does the continuing study of historical theology offer us? Most obviously, it offers access to records of the accumulated experience of Orthodox Christians. It may provide unexpected and immediate insight into contemporary problems, or open uncommon vantages onto the modern world. Access to the

---

patristic heritage of Orthodoxy, ancient and medieval and modern, enables us to enrich and to transmit that heritage in its complexity. A robust and complex engagement with that heritage will tell us about the present in a way that mere repetition of ancient slogans will never do.

The systematic study of languages, history, philosophy, and cultures is vital to accessing and thus to perpetuating patristic theology. These endeavors can be undertaken as a spiritual discipline, since success in them involves the cultivation of virtues that are as valuable to Christian living as to theological research. The hallmarks of good scholarship in patristics are carefulness, humility, patience, honesty, and integrity. These dispositions promote understanding and facilitate communication. And this is true irrespective of how much formal training the student of patristic theology has acquired. Not everyone has the time, desire, or aptitude to undertake advanced study in those areas. Nor is it necessary that everyone should. The mechanisms by which the patristic heritage is available to us are manifold. Being a scholar is not prerequisite to being involved in the conservation, transmission, and augmentation of that heritage. We are all called to witness faithfully to God, sharing in joyous fellowship with God's beloved ones throughout the ages.